DRUGS, CRIME, AND VIOLENCE

From Trafficking to Treatment

Howard Rahtz

Introduction by Jack W. Brown

Hamilton Books
A member of
The Rowman & Littlefield Publishing Group
Lanham · Boulder · New York · Toronto · Plymouth, UK

Copyright © 2012 by
Hamilton Books
4501 Forbes Boulevard
Suite 200
Lanham, Maryland 20706
Hamilton Books Acquisitions Department (301) 459-3366

10 Thornbury Road
Plymouth PL6 7PP
United Kingdom

All rights reserved
Printed in the United States of America
British Library Cataloging in Publication Information Available

Library of Congress Control Number: 2012941712
ISBN: 978-0-7618-5967-3 (paperback : alk. paper)
eISBN: 978-0-7618-5968-0

∞™ The paper used in this publication meets the minimum
requirements of American National Standard for Information
Sciences—Permanence of Paper for Printed Library Materials,
ANSI Z39.48-1992

Dedication

Thanks to Caroline and Christine, my daughters, who also served as my editors putting this book into the proper form; to my wife Kathy for tolerating the chaos this project created in our house; and Denny, for those welcome trips to the golf course where I was able to rewind and recover. I love you guys.

Table of Contents

Preface		vii
Acknowledgements		ix
Introduction by Jack W. Brown, Ph.D.		xi
Chapter 1	Drugs, Crime and Violence	1
Chapter 2	The Illegal Drug Market	10
Chapter 3	Learning From the Past	21
Chapter 4	Policy Options	38
Chapter 5	An International Perspective	52
Chapter 6	Drug Abuse—The Damage Done	69
Chapter 7	Addiction: The Driving Force behind the Illegal Market	82
Chapter 8	Marijuana—The Cartel's Cash Cow	90
Chapter 9	From Trafficking to Treatment	99
Chapter 10	The Costs of Policy Paralysis	111
Chapter 11	A New Direction	117
Bibliography		128

Preface

On my retirement from the Cincinnati Police Department in 2007, I began writing this book on drug policy. I have a somewhat unique perspective on the drug problem as I am one of only a handful of people who have worked on both sides of the drug supply-demand equation. I began my career as a counselor in a Methadone Program and spent nearly twenty years working with addicts and their families. At age 42, I began a second career as a Cincinnati Police Officer, rising to the rank of Captain and retiring as head of the department's Vice Unit.

Originally, I intended to write about local community response to drug issues. Law enforcement and the treatment community have more in common than they realize and I thought a more coordinated effort at the grassroots level might have a significant impact on neighborhood drug problems. But as my research into our country's drug problems expanded, I grew more intrigued with the broader illegal drug market and its role as the catalyst of violence, from the street drug markets in our cities to the escalating drug war on the Mexican border.

Our response to date could only be described as the same old same old—more border agents, more police, more arrests and bigger jails with a measure of drug treatment and prevention thrown in. Robert Stutman, former head of the New York DEA office, nicely captured the insanity of our current response—"Build a 12-foot wall around the U.S. The old joke is it takes dope peddlers 60 seconds to realize a 13-foot ladder gets over a 12-foot wall. Then what? Build a 13-foot wall?"

I am now convinced that with some significant policy moves, we can destroy the financial underpinnings of the illegal drug market. Like any other business enterprise, the illegal drug market cannot exist without its customer base. We can take two policy steps siphoning off the majority of its customers.

The first is to legalize marijuana. Moving marijuana to a legal status takes 30-40% of the customers of the drug market and transitions them to the legitimate economy. The impact of such a move on the illegal drug market is beyond dispute. The medical marijuana market in California has already impacted drug traffickers as legally grown and distributed marijuana competes with the illegal market. Law enforcement and other observers note that the competition from even this limited legal market has eroded illegal trafficking more than 50 years of harsh laws and millions of arrests.

Legalizing marijuana also accomplishes what policy-makers refer to as "separation of the markets." Marijuana buyers now participate in a market where access to other drugs, crack, heroin and methamphetamine, are not only available, but actively pushed. Removing easy access to these drugs will mean fewer users and related problems.

Legalization represents the potential for significant revenue to cash-strapped government at all levels. The marijuana market, from growers to wholesalers and retail distribution network, constitutes a major economic entity. A tax policy that earmarks a portion of these funds for drug prevention and treatment would be a reasonable option.

While the legalization of marijuana would strike a blow at the cartels, other policy changes can further marginalize these traffickers. These changes all target drug addicts, the lifeblood of the illegal market. With some modification of drug laws and expansion of treatment resources, I believe we can move substantially more addicts out of the drug market and into drug treatment. Without these heavy consumers, the illegal market would wither.

This book is now the rationale and prescription for a new approach to our drug problem. While the ongoing debate over drug policy is often loud and vociferous, there are very few Americans who are defending the status quo. From citizens of the states which have approved medical marijuana to voters in Breckenridge, Colorado who in 2009 voted to legalize marijuana, Americans across the country are voting their discontent with current policy. Our choice as policy makers is to react to the change or lead it. It is time to begin a national discussion on the choices we face.

Howard Rahtz
March, 2012

Acknowledgements

I owe particular thanks to Lieutenants Art Frey and Bob Ruebusch for their patience and generosity in teaching me about drug trafficking. Thanks to Dave Logan and Nan Franks for their continuing leadership in battling the addictions problem in Cincinnati. And I also want to acknowledge all the police officers, counselors and the multitude of addictions professionals who work so relentlessly in combating our drug problems. The courage and persistence they show every day is an inspiration and they do a remarkable job in dangerous and trying conditions.

And to my friend and colleague, Jack W. Brown, for his introduction and his editing assistance.

Introduction by Jack W. Brown, Ph.D.

During my twenty-five years in and around the justice system as a practitioner and as a professor, I have witnessed first-hand the profound impact illegal drugs have had on America's citizens. Whether male or female, rich or poor, black or white, educated or uneducated, young or old, *no one* in our country is beyond the reach of crime, drugs, and violence. As we find ourselves at the beginning of the second decade of the twenty-first century, nearly thirty years after the abolishment of the LEAA, we look back at a wave of street crime rivaled only by the era of Prohibition.

As cocaine distribution made its way into south Florida in the early 1980s and rapidly moved north into New York City and west across Texas and into California, crime proliferated to the point where all America could do to make sense of it all was to, of all things, glamorize the drugs, guns, and violence associated with the cocaine trade by putting it front-and-center on the main medium of the time, television, in the form of a prime-time "let's start the weekend off right" show known as "Miami Vice." After nearly six years on the air, Miami Vice, with its focus on flashy cars, sex, drug cartels, murder, and cash, gave way to its successor, "Law and Order." Thus Americans were introduced to the competing ends of the late 20th century social landscape: flash, cash, and crime versus law, order, and justice.

While solidifying the victory of "law" over "vice" as concerns the preference of Americans for the structure of the foundation of civil society, the dawn of the "Homeland Security" era in 2001, ironically, supplanted the nation's focus on street crime to such a degree that street-level crimes, and their prevailing influences, made their way from the front page of newspapers to the back page; from the lead story on the six o'clock news to the final segment before sign-off. In colleges and universities, courses such as "Probation and

Parole" and "Community Corrections" gave way to courses in "Terrorism," "Cybercrime," and "Homeland Security."

In concert with social and academic changes in response to street-level drug crime at the dawn of the 21st century, American society witnessed a change in the preference of its citizens as concerns their drug of choice. Gone were the days of law enforcement working to eradicate the effects of marijuana, cocaine, or crack. Law enforcement was faced with the reality that Americans no longer simply fancied one illegal drug for a couple of years before "switching brands;" officers were faced with the stark reality that Americans, while still routinely procuring and using marijuana and cocaine, were also looking to involve themselves with heroin, crystal meth, OxyContin, and inhalants. As well, law enforcement routinely found drug-related calls-for-service as likely to be in suburbia as in the inner-city; as likely to be to a street corner as to a college dorm room; as likely to be an arrest of a street criminal as a housewife.

Along with this rise in drug-related street crime and America's permanent focus on law and order via its dedication to Homeland Security came two realities the American justice system was simply not prepared to handle: overcrowding of the courts, and overcrowding of jails and prisons. As the court dockets and the carceral facilities began to overflow, the American economy began to slowdown, thus creating an economic crisis as concerns how taxpayers were going to continue to support the ever-growing criminal population that was a result of their preferred policy of social control—arrest, prosecute, incarcerate.

Astute observers such as Howard Rahtz see that the drug epidemic of the past twenty-five years and the punishment philosophies that followed simply will not work in the 21st century, especially when one considers the sheer numbers of drug addicts in America today, America's current economic state, and the shocking state of the population of America's court dockets and America's jails and prisons. The DEA and the NIDA seem to be at cross-purposes. The time is right for America to move from "law and order" to "justice and society."

In his new book, Howard Rahtz provides the reader with an excellent history of the major players in the illegal drug trade and how their efforts support crime in America. He also examines a topic too often underserved by other authors writing on the topic of illegal drugs, namely, the role of marijuana in the past, current, and future legal and economic realities of America. In chapters such as "Drug Abuse" and "Addiction," Rahtz effortlessly moves the reader from an understanding of drugs, crime, and violence to an understanding of the role addiction and treatment currently plays—and must continue to play— in 21st century criminal justice.

This book is an excellent look at the inner-workings of the past quarter-century of the foundation of crime in America. In addition to providing the reader with a clear understanding of the history of the development of the illegal drug market in America and its legal and economic influence on the shaping of American society, Howard Rahtz concludes this fast-paced read with a well-defined and clear recommendation for a fundamental change in the focus of

American criminal justice policy. I have no doubt other authors will follow Rahtz's lead in calling for smarter penal policy to effect deliverance of justice to all Americans that recognizes them first and foremost not as criminals in need of punishment, but as people in need of treatment.

Jack W. Brown, Ph.D.
Dean- Division of Justice Studies
Beckfield College

Chapter 1

Drugs, Crime and Violence

> *"America's public enemy number one in the United States is drug abuse. In order to fight and defeat this enemy, it is necessary to wage a new, all-out offensive."*
>
> President Richard M. Nixon
> June 17, 1971

For nearly 50 years, the United States has been involved in what has commonly been termed the "War on Drugs." Over the years, the primary enemy in this war has changed from marijuana and LSD in the 1960's to heroin and cocaine in the 70's, to crack in the 80's. As the crack epidemic waned in the 90's, methamphetamine moved front and center and more recently, ecstasy and a resurgence of heroin have captured the headlines.

Casualties in the war are uncountable. Thousands of people have been killed in drug related violence, millions more have been jailed, and billions of dollars have been spent at home and abroad in an attempt to control the illegal drug trade. American cities are plagued by drug violence. Local governments are straining to provide funding for police, jails and treatment programs overwhelmed by drug offenders. Less visible are the families silently coping with the addiction of a loved one, a suicide or overdose death of a son or daughter, or the death of a family member in a senseless incident of drug-related violence.

Over the past 40 years, I have served as a foot soldier in the war on drugs. Coming out of graduate school in the early 1970's, I worked as a counselor in one of the first Methadone Programs serving heroin addicts in the state of Ohio. For the next 20 years I worked in a variety of treatment and prevention programs, all with the same goal—assisting addicts and their families. In 1988, at the age of 42, I became a Cincinnati Police Officer. Serving as a beat cop in some of the city's most troubled neighborhoods during the height of the crack epidemic provided a view of the drug problem far different from that seen from behind a counselor's desk. Years later, at the end of my police career, I was placed in charge of the department's Vice Control Unit, with primary responsibility for the city's drug enforcement. With a staff of committed and talented officers, a close partnership with federal authorities, and an emphasis on mid-level traffickers, we seized record quantities of drugs and money from arrested dealers. Despite these successes, it was clear to me our impact on the problem was minimal at best.

This frustration is one shared by police, drug counselors, educators and all the others engaged in the nation's drug war. While criminal justice and addictions professionals experience small wins every day, the country's drug problem rolls on. It changes shape as new drugs, or old ones in new disguises, take center stage. The drug problem is implicated in much of the country's street violence and treats as a small irritant the thousands of users and dealers arrested. It adapts to efforts at interdiction and coldly murders those who would threaten the business. It uses its vast income to support terror activities, to corrupt government officials and to sabotage legitimate businesses.

It would be difficult to find a problem more resistant to change. The historical effort to solve the drug problem encompasses a lengthy litany of initiatives ranging from well-intentioned media campaigns, to periodically declared wars featuring get-tough politicians posturing impotently in the face of the devastation drug-related violence has had on our communities. As a nation, we continue to struggle with the development of a rational approach to the problem. The search for a consensus approach often fractures the community into opposing camps with little tolerance of other viewpoints.

I am convinced we can do better. Our current "war on drugs" policy framework is in large part either ineffective or, worse, counterproductive. The complexity of the drug problem demands a coordinated and rational approach free of the simplistic sloganeering characterizing much of our past efforts. The first step in more effectively dealing with the drug problem is a deeper understanding of the dimensions of the problem we are facing.

THE AMERICAN DRUG PROBLEM

From the threat of international terrorism, to crime on the streets, to the troubled family down the block, drug problems infect every area of American life. In a sometimes obvious, but often subtle fashion, America's appetite for drugs fuels the most serious problems bedeviling the country.

The illegal drug business is truly a global enterprise generating an estimated $500 billion annually; more than the international oil and gas industry combined and twice the revenue of the global auto industry.[1] It supports international terrorism and poses a serious threat to governments around the world. U.S. intelligence authorities list over 125 countries involved in drug trafficking[2] and the United Nations estimates that worldwide illegal drug sales are larger than the gross national product of 88% of the world's countries.[3]

Afghanistan is now the world's largest producer of opium and accounts for over 90% of the world's supply of heroin.[4] The 2006 opium crop in Afghanistan was at a record high with much of the production occurring in the country's southern provinces under the watch of Taliban Insurgents.[5] The 2007 crop exceeded 2006's record total by over a third and U.S. military commanders predict the 2008 crop will be even larger.[6] Proceeds from the Afghani drug trafficking provide crucial support for the Taliban.

Columbia remains the world's largest source of cocaine representing over 50% of the world's coca production.[7] While the Columbian coca crop dropped off slightly from 2005 to 2006, the decline was offset by increased cultivation in Peru and Bolivia. Drug seizures of cocaine intercepted en route from Latin America fell from 262 metric tons in 2006 to 210 tons in 2007, a decline of 20%. The 2007 totals were the lowest in five years, a decline the U.S. authorities attribute to changes in traffickers' tactics. Admiral Mike Mullen, Chairman of the Joint Chiefs of Staff, noted the drug smugglers are finding new ways of avoiding detection by the authorities, stating, "The bad guy is moving faster than we're moving."[8]

Admiral Mullen's concerns were highlighted when in late 2007, a secret shipyard was discovered in a Columbian jungle. The facility was believed to be building submarines designed for drug smuggling, verifying recent intelligence that traffickers were building submarines to help them evade Coast Guard patrols.[9]

The situation is likely to worsen over the next few years. In November of 2008, Bolivian officials gave United States Drug Enforcement Agency (DEA) officers three months to leave the country. This action followed by only a few months the call by the Ecuadorian government for the DEA to leave that country. Both Bolivia and Ecuador are important links in the drug trafficking network.[10]

Closer to home, drug gangs and violence pose an escalating threat on the Mexican border. Rising drug violence in 2009 brought Secretary of State Hillary Clinton to Mexico with a $700 million assistance package that included hundreds of new federal agents assigned to the Mexican border to stem the flow of drugs into the US. In commenting on the violence, Clinton called it "horrific" while acknowledging that the demand for drugs in the US is fueling the violence.[11]

While the violence began to capture the attention of both the media and public officials in 2009, it has been escalating for the last several years. Drug related violence in Mexico has accounted for an estimated 40,000 murders since Mexican President Felipe Calderon declared war on drug traffickers in 2006.[12] While much of violence stems from rival groups competing for control of the drug trade, police and military officials as well as media representatives have also been targeted. In May of 2007, Lugo Felix, the newly appointed head of a Drug Intelligence Unit in the National Attorney General's office was shot and killed in a street ambush. The killing was viewed as a direct attack on President Felipe Calderon's campaign against drug traffickers.

The drug violence has been widespread. In Monterrey, on one Saturday night in February, 2011, eight people were killed in an episode of drug violence. The next night, the Monterrey Police Chief, Homero Salcido, was ambushed and killed.[13] Acapulco, a popular spot for tourists from around the world, has been the site of some of the most serious violence. In February of 2007 armed men staged simultaneous raids on two Acapulco offices of the state attorney general, killing seven state workers. In 2006, the heads of six alleged victims of traffickers were found in the resort area, leading the federal government to dispatch 7,000 federal troops to assist local authorities.[14]

The drug-related violence has grown to encompass attacks including the kidnapping and murder of journalists. In an incident in February of 2006, two masked gunmen with assault rifles and grenades entered the offices of El Manana newspaper in Nuevo Laredo, tossed grenades and fired rifles. Jaime Orozco Tey, a reporter investigating the drug cartels, was wounded. A few days later, the newspaper's editor announced the paper would no longer investigate stories related to the drug cartels.[15]

The violence shows no sign of abating. In July of 2010, drug cartel gunmen stormed a party in the Northern Mexico town of Torreon and killed 18 people. The dead included 12 males and six females, four of them teenagers. The party massacre followed May gunfire targeted at a Torreon television station and the offices of a Torreon newspaper. Authorities link the killings to the ongoing battle for control of the drug trade between competing drug gangs, the Gulf and the Sinaloa cartels.[16]

On July 18, 2010, in a disturbing new twist in the violence, gang members deployed a car bomb in a sophisticated operation targeting police in Ciudad Juarez, scene of some of the worst drug violence in Mexico. Drug gang members dropped a mortally wounded man dressed in a police uniform at an intersection, calling in a false report of a wounded officer. As federal police and paramedics rushed to the scene, the killers detonated a car bomb.[17]

Drug violence along the Mexican border has spilled over into the U.S. with incidents intensifying the debate on immigration and border security. Drug related kidnappings have become a common occurrence in both Phoenix and San Diego. Phoenix police reported more than 340 kidnappings in 2007 where the victims were involved in drug or immigrant smuggling. In some cases, victims' "bound and bullet-riddled bodies have been found in the desert."[18]

Particularly troubling has been the increasing willingness of traffickers to directly confront and threaten U. S. Law Enforcement. In January of 2006, Hudspeth County (Texas) deputies engaged in a border standoff with men armed with assault rifles and dressed in Mexican military uniforms. According to Hudspeth County Sheriff Arvin West, a few weeks after the incident, individuals identified as drug dealers confronted some Hudspeth County Deputies at the deputies' homes and threatened their families. West believes the incident is an example of the federal government's inattention to border security. "Our borders are wide open for anyone, terrorists as well and the death toll keeps growing," he said.[19]

Sheriff West is not alone in his concern about terrorists exploiting the porous southern border. Robert Grenier, a former head of the U.S. Central Intelligence Agency's Counterterrorism Center, believes Hamas and Hezbullah agents may be setting up operations in Mexico as a base for terrorist strikes in the U.S. Speaking in Mexico in February of 2007, Grenier, who now runs The Kroll Security Agency, stated the terrorists could use existing drug trafficking networks to facilitate future attacks.[20]

Grenier's fears were confirmed in 2009 when U.S. officials acknowledged that the terrorist group Hezbollah was using Mexican narcotics smuggling routes to finance its operations. Recently retired DEA official Michael Braun stated Hezbollah relies on "the same criminal weapons smugglers, document traffickers and transportation experts as the drug cartels." Braun's comments were verified by various US law enforcement, counterterrorism and defense experts.[21]

Perhaps the most chilling connection between terrorism and drug trafficking is the one identified by Paul Williams, an investigative journalist who has also worked as an FBI Consultant. Williams is the author of a book on Osama Bin Ladin's quest to obtain nuclear weapons entitled *Osama's Revenge: the Next 9/11: What the Media and the Government Haven't Told You*. In the book, Williams claims Bin Laden purchased 20 suitcase-sized nuclear devices from the Chechen Mafia, paying $30 million in cash and two tons of heroin. Al-Qaida's leader was a major drug producer and trafficker in Afghanistan. "It is the drug money, not the Bin Laden family fortune, that is the financial engine for al-Qaida," said Williams.[22]

Recent reports not only verify the Al Qaeda-drug connection but corroborate an alarming new alliance between Colombian drug lords and Al Qaeda terrorists in West Africa. DEA official Jay Bergman confirmed new intelligence in Yemen substantiated the rumored connection. "As suggested by the recent arrest of three alleged Al Qaeda operatives, the expansion of cocaine trafficking through West Africa has provided the venue for an unholy alliance between South American narco-terrorists and Islamic extremists," said Bergman.[23]

Drugs also fuel much of the criminal violence within the U.S. A quick scan of news reports paints a graphic picture of shootings and homicides almost invariably labeled as "drug related." In recent history, experts point to the simultaneous increase in violent crime and the explosion of the crack epidemic in the late 1980's and early 90's as clear evidence of the drug and violence connection.[24]

While there is widespread agreement on the connection between drugs and crime, the dimensions and nature of the connection remains the subject of heated debate. The factors underlying criminal violence are complicated and the precise role of drugs in the violence is uncertain but the reality of the drug and violence connection cannot be denied.

Recent research sheds some light on the nature and extent of drug related violence. In 2004, as part of the National Crime Victimization Survey, victims of violence were asked to describe whether they believed the offender in their particular crime had been drinking or using drugs. Approximately 30% of the victims reported the offender was using drugs or alcohol at the time of the offense.[25] In a similar survey of college students who had been victims of violent crime, 41% reported the offender using drugs or alcohol at the time of the offense. Approximately two in five of all rape/sexual assaults and nearly 25% of all robberies against a college student were committed by an offender thought to be using drugs or alcohol.[26]

Surveys of prison inmates also support the significant role of drug involvement in crime. A study of state and federal inmates in 2004 found just under 20% of the prisoners stating they committed their current offense to support a drug habit.[27] Another study compared the drug related crime of property crime offenders and violent offenders, finding the violent offenders less likely to commit their crimes for drug money than property crime offenders.[28]

Drug involvement in violent crime, particularly homicide, is viewed as much more of a factor in large urban areas. While the homicide rate has dropped dramatically in New York and to a lesser extent in Chicago, other cities are experiencing a surge in homicides. In 2006, police chiefs of many of the country's major urban centers came together to warn of a "gathering storm of crime" in American cities. Their report, published by the Police Executive Research Foundation (PERF), documents a significant reversal of the declining crime trends of the late 90's and into the 21st century. In 2005, violent crime in America recorded the largest single-year increase in 14 years. Eleven cities, among them Orlando, FL, Cincinnati, OH, Trenton NJ, Boston, MA, and Richmond, CA (a suburb of Oakland), all reported homicides at record highs. Police chiefs in these cities blame a trifecta of gangs, drugs and guns for the violence.[29] Speculation about the underlying factors in the crime increase included the usual suspects—street gang involvement, easy access to guns, violent juvenile offenders, lack of social services, a criminal justice re-

---

Street Violence

On May 10, 2011, 38-year old Santonio Furr was shot and killed in Cincinnati's Over-the-Rhine area. In a city where the homicide rate exploded over the last several years, Furr's death was notable due only to the fact he was holding a 14-month old infant in his arms at the time of the murder. Furr had a long history of drug involvement and was in court the morning of his murder to face his most recent charges. The 14-month old was not injured in the incident.[30]

volving door and the litany of social ills that plague crime-infested neighborhoods. Much of the current criminal violence in the U.S., particularly in urban areas, is related to the drug trade. In the complicated interplay of the lethal mix of drugs, gangs, and guns, it is difficult, if not impossible, to precisely calculate the role of each.

The city of Newark, New Jersey, typifies the situation in many cities. After a decline in the city's murder rate in the early years of the 21st century, homicides spiked in 2006, and Newark suffered six homicides in just the first few weeks of 2007. Mayor Corey Booker announced the formation of a new narcotics squad to coordinate an aggressive assault on drug dealing, which the police have long tied to a large share of the city's homicides and gun violence. Newark Police Director Garry McCarthy said "The vast majority of violence comes from narcotics."[31]

The particular mix of factors likely differs from city to city. Dr. O'Dell Owens, the Hamilton County, Ohio, Coroner, has presided over Cincinnati's recent record-level homicides. While recognizing the variety of factors in the homicide issue, Owens states bluntly "Drugs are fueling 90% of the city's homicides."[32]

DISCUSSION

While violence is the most visible manifestation of America's drug problem, it is unfortunately the tip of the iceberg. The effects of America's drug problem ricochet through the country resulting in escalating health-care costs, economic damage to neighborhoods and a tremendous financial burden suffered by local and state governments struggling to control the problem. Yet the higher costs are the incalculable damage to the families of America; the thousands of children abused and neglected by addicted parents; the sons and daughters lost to drug overdoses or street violence; and the ongoing parade of addicts crowding court systems, emergency rooms and social services.

Only the most determined optimist believes the War on Drugs a success. In our War on Drugs, the United States spends more money and incarcerates more of its citizens than any other country in the world. Based on addiction and use rates, we have little to show for it. Gil Kerlikowske, the current federal Drug Czar, in a nicely understated tone, notes "not many people think the drug war is a success."[33]

Trying to understand our nation's drug problem is akin to the story of the six blind men each touching a different part of the elephant and describing it to the others. The problem does look much different to the street cop, to the drug counselor, to the emergency room doctor, and to the immigration authority. The police struggle to stop the street violence, the counselor supports the addicts looking to escape their addiction, and medical people are overwhelmed with the dead and dying flooding the emergency room. Each brings a certain perspective in seeking an end to the carnage.

A new strategy to directly confront the cartels and deprive them of the revenue supporting the violence, has the potential to bring those now engaged on various fronts, in our futile war on drugs, together. While the mix of drug policy options which would be effective in reducing America's drug problem remain the subject of intense debate, there is little doubt a strategy which would choke off revenue to both international cartel members and local drug dealers would find wide acceptance.

Making this new direction a reality will require an understanding of the illegal drug market. A review of past attempts to control drug problems, including alcohol prohibition, and a scan of drug control measures in other countries, also will shed some light on effective countermeasures.

The single most important element in understanding the new direction is the role of addiction in supporting the illegal market. While experts will quarrel about the precise definition of addiction and use terms like drug abuse or psychological dependency to describe slightly differing problem patterns, the fact is the core feature of problem drugs is the grip with which they ensnare a percentage of those who are using them. It is addicts, those whose lives begin to revolve around their drug use, who fuel the illegal drug market. Without an effective policy addressing their addiction problems, attempts to suppress the illegal drug market will be futile.

NOTES

1. United Nations Office on Drugs and Crime. (1998). *Economic and Social Consequences of Drug Abuse and Illicit Trafficking.* New York, NY: UNODCCP. Retrieved from http://www.unodc.org/pdf/technical_series_1998-01-01_1.pdf.
2. Central Intelligence Agency. (2007). *Field Listing: Elicit drugs* [Data file]. Retrieved from http://www.cia.gov/library/publications/the-world-factbook/.
3. United Nations Office on Drugs and Crime. (2007). *2007 World Drug Report* [Data file]. Available from http://www.unodc.org/.
4. Ibid.
5. Jane's Information Group. (2006 November 15). "Afghanistan's Narcotics-Fuelled Insurgency." Retrieved from http://www.janes.com/.
6. "U.S. Expects Record Poppy Crop in Afghanistan." (2008, January 3). *USA Today.* Retrieved from http://www.usatoday.com/news/world/2008-01-02-afghanistan-poppy_N.htm.
7. United Nations on Drugs and Crime, 2007.
8. Burns, R. (2007 January 15). "Seizures of Cocaine Shipments Fall Off in '07." *Greenville News.*
9. Harlow, J. (2007, November 11). "Drug Smugglers Use Submarines." *Times Online.* Retrieved from http://www.timesonline.co.uk/tol/news/world/us_and_americas/article2848238.ec.
10. Miller, S. (2008, November 11). "Bolivia, Ecuador, Venezuela Evict U.S. Drug Warriors." *The Christian Science Monitor.* Retrieved from http://www.csmonitor.com.
11. Strobel, W. P. (2009, March 27). "Clinton Says US Shares Responsibility for Mexico's Drug Violence." *The Christian Science Monitor.* Retrieved from http://www.csmonitor.com/2009/0327/p99s01-woam.html.

12. Thompson, Ginger (2011, December 4). "US drug agents launder profits of Mexican cartels." Cincinnati, Enquirer, A7.
13. Chron.com. "More drug violence, plus reports of 8500 orphans in Juarez." Retrieved from http://blog.chron.com/newswatch/2011/02/mexico-more-drug-violence-plus-reports-of-8500-orphans-in-juarez/.
14. Para, N. (2007, February 7). "Seven State Workers Slain in Acapulco." *Associated Press*.
15. Carter, S. A. & Barrera, E. (2006, February 28). "Slayings Tied to Cartels." *San Bernadino County News*.
16. Villalba, Oscar (2010). "Officials Say Gunmen Kill Seventeen at Party in Mexico." Associated Press, July 18, 2010. Retrieved from http://news.yahoo.com/s/ap/20100718/.
17. Ibid.
18. Billeaud, J. (2008, January 12). "Kidnappings for Ransom Move North of the Border." *Cincinnati Enquirer*.
19. Carter & Barrera (2006, February 28) "Slayings tied to cartels." San Bernadino County News.
20. Nahmais, R. (2007, November 2). "Expert: Hamas, Hezbollah Cells may be Active in Mexico." *Ynet News*. Retrieved from http://www.ynetnews.com.
21. Carter, S. A. (2009, March 27). "Hezbollah Uses Mexican Drug Routes into U.S." *Washington Times*.
22. Stogel, S. (2004, July 14). "Al-Qaida has Nuclear Weapons Inside U.S." *NewsMax*. Available from http://www.newsmax.com/index.html.
23. Bronstein, Hugh (2010, January 5). "Colombia Rebels, Al Qaeda in "Unholy" Drug Alliance." Reuters.com.
24. Caulkins, J. P., Reuter, P.H., Iguchi, M.Y. & Chiesa, J. (2003). "Drug Use and Drug Policy Futures: Insights from a Colloquium." Retrieved from http://www.rand.org/pubs/issue_papers/IP246/.
25. Bureau of Justice Statistics. (2006, October). *Drug Use and Dependence, State and Federal Prisoners, 2004* [Data file]. Retrieved from http://www.ojp.usdoj.gov/bjs.
26. Bureau of Justice Statistics. (2003, December). *Violent Victimization of College Students: National Crime Victimization Survey 1995-2000* [Data file]. Retrieved from http://www.ojp.usdoj.gov/bjs.
27. Bureau of Justice Statistics. (2006) *Drug Use and Dependence*. Retrieved from http://www.ojp.usdoj.gov/bjs/pub.
28. Bureau of Justice Statistics. (1999, January). *Substance Abuse and Treatment, State and Federal Prisoners, 1999* [Data file]. Retrieved from http://www.ojp.usdoj.gov/bjs/pub.
29. Police Executive Research Forum. (2006). *"A Gathering Storm – Violent Crime in America."* Retrieved from http://www.policeforum.org.
30. http://www.local12.com/news/local/story/Man-Murdered-in-Over-the-Rhine-While-Holding/ElMZQY5h_kWujazHOXLauA.cspx. May 18, 2011
31. Lueck, T. J. (2007, January 8). "As Newark Mayor Readies Crime Fight, Toll Rises." *The New York Times*. Retrieved from http://www.nytimes.com/2007/01/08/nyregion/08newark.html.
32. Weathers, W. (2007, January 13). "Homicide Record Just Got Worse." *Cincinnati Post*, p. B1.
33. Will, George. (2009, October 29). "Gil Kerlikowske's Reality Check In The Drug War." The Washington Post Retrieved from http://www.washingtonpost.com/wp-n/content/article/2009/10/28/AR2009102803801.html.

Chapter 2

The Illegal Drug Market

> *U.S. officials see a strategic problem with their neighbor's surging violence and unstable judicial and law enforcement systems. Mexican officials blame that instability on the insatiable U.S. demand for lucrative and illegal narcotics.*
>
> *(Mendoza, 2010)*

The illegal drug market consists of a business with an international reach, spanning the globe from Afghanistan to the street corners of large and small American communities. The business includes farmers raising the marijuana, coca leaf or opium poppies, processing operations converting the raw material into the drug product, transportation and distribution networks that deliver the drug from processing operations to wholesalers in the states, and street level retailers passing the drug directly to the user.

The basic business model varies with particular drugs but the international business of drug trafficking has shown itself as a nimble and well-entrenched operation undeterred by law enforcement efforts at every level. If the international drug business were a monolithic entity, it would perhaps be more vulnerable to enforcement efforts. But it is much more like a multi-headed group of organizations each attempting to carve out a piece of the profit pie. A Rand Corporation report on the global drug market over the past 10 years reached the sad conclusion that despite significant international efforts, there was "no evidence that the global drug problem was reduced during the ...period from 1998-2007."[1] The report documents the adaptability of the illegal market responding to the variety of efforts to suppress it and describes a number of unintended negative consequences that accompany some of the suppression strategies.

The value of a drug inflates as it proceeds up the distribution chain. A quantity of coca leaf worth $650 to the Columbian farmer retails as 100 mg. of pure cocaine worth $120,000 dollars on the streets of Chicago. Heroin makes a similar journey from farmer to the street. Opium worth $550 in Afghanistan increases in value nearly 250 fold by the time it is processed as heroin and reaches the addict on the corner.[2] Part of the value increase is related to the length of the product chain for these two drugs. This contrasts with marijuana and methamphetamine where the supply chain is less arduous.

Marijuana and methamphetamine take a less torturous route from raw product to the user due primarily to the dominance of Mexican traffickers. Mexican DTOs (Drug Trafficking Organizations) have continued to increase the amount of marijuana smuggled into the United States while at the same time moving to establish large-scale marijuana farming operations inside the U.S. Marijuana production in Mexico jumped an estimated 59% from 2003 to 2009 with significantly larger amounts smuggled into the United.States.[3] The amount of marijuana produced domestically has also been escalating as well. Domestic production not only eliminates the risk of cross-border smuggling but also lowers transportation costs and provides easier access to the end customer.[4]

Marijuana grow operations discovered in U.S. national parks have become almost common-place. In 2009, authorities found 14,500 marijuana plants in Pike National Forest in Colorado. DEA officials attributed the operation to Mexican DTOs. According to officials, illegal immigrants were imported to work the operations which can be established at low cost yet bring in significant revenue. In the first few months of 2009 authorities discovered large grow operations in California, Idaho, and Colorado with an estimated value of $55 million. Growers have been operating in a number of National Parks including Sequoia and Redwood national forests.[5]

The consequences of these operations extend beyond the drug issue. Authorities bemoan the environmental impact including toxic chemicals contaminating the ground, clear-cutting of the land for the grow operation, and mountains of debris left behind when the site is abandoned. Environmental safety is hardly a concern to the traffickers, and authorities believe a drug cartel grow operation ignited a fire in July of 2009 that destroyed 88,000 acres in the Los Padres National Forest.[6]

Mexican DTOs are also responsible for the bulk of the methamphetamine smuggled into the U.S. Based on drug seizures at the border, authorities estimate the amount of methamphetamines smuggled into the U.S. decreased during 2006 and 2007 but jumped dramatically again in 2009 as traffickers adapted to Mexican government restrictions on pseudoephedrine and ephedrine imports. The two substances are precursor chemicals used to produce meth but traffickers have moved to the use of other chemicals contributing to their upsurge in production.[7]

Yet even the short-lived loss of production in Mexico was offset by increased domestic production, particularly an increase in so-called meth super-labs in California.[8]

The bulk of the illegal drugs smuggled into the U.S. arrive overland across the Mexican border and to a smaller extent, across the Canadian border. The drugs come in commercial trucks and vans, private cars and trucks, in all terrain vehicles and even on foot. Smuggling by sea routes is also a popular method with cruise ships, container vehicles, fishing boats and even small self-propelled submarine type vessels used to move drugs. Movement by air represents only a small portion of the current drug smuggling picture.[9]

Once in the United States, drugs are stored in houses, ranches, trailers, and warehouses and then packaged and shipped to various U.S. distribution points. Traffickers will use commercial trucks, private vehicles, commercial cargo companies (FedEx, UPS) and the U.S. Postal Service to move the drugs. The movement of drugs to markets within the country follows the nation's major highway routes. Sometimes the drugs are moved in large quantities but in other instances, the transportation movement consists of individuals buying a smaller quantity of drugs in a major market with the goal of reselling the drugs in his hometown.

The bulk of drug network activity occurs unnoticed by the public. Every day, as commuters zip through the roadways intersecting their communities, they pass drug couriers and dealers moving their product towards its final street market destination. When the drug finally reaches the street corner, packaged for consumer sale, the scope of the problem appears. The Rand Corporation study estimates 90% of the total drug trafficking network operates at the retail end. The retail sales operation includes a large number of low-level personnel, some acting as lookouts and others assigned the hand to hand transactions as directed by higher-level dealers who keep themselves removed from the actual deals.[10] It is the street corner market where drug-related violence and disorder directly threaten community safety.

Where open-air drug markets flourish, safety and resident quality of life are diminished. Dealers take over local parks, intimidate residents and harm legitimate businesses. A partial list of the problems generated by illegal street markets includes:

- traffic congestion,
- noise (from traffic and people),
- disorderly conduct,
- begging,
- loitering,
- vandalism,
- drug use and littering (discarded drug paraphernalia),
- criminal damage to property,
- prostitution,
- robbery,
- residential and commercial burglary,
- theft from motor vehicles,

- fencing stolen goods,
- weapons offenses, and
- assaults and homicides.[11]

This somewhat antiseptic list of drug market problems obscures the level of violence and tragedy that permeates American neighborhoods. In Chicago, where the homicides of schoolchildren are attracting national attention, officials are struggling to understand a level of violence shocking even by big-city standards. "There's simply too many gangs, too many guns and too many drugs on the streets" says Chicago Police Superintendent Jody Weis.[12] Drugs provide the financial fuel that supports the gangs, that buys the guns. Elijah Anderson, in his book on inner-city violence, *Code of the Street*, writes:

> In the impoverished inner-city neighborhood, the drug trade is everywhere, and it becomes ever more difficult to separate the drug culture from the experience of poverty. The neighborhood is sprinkled with crack dens located in abandoned buildings or in someone's home. On corner after corner, young men peddle drugs the way a newsboy peddles papers. To those who pass their brief inspection, they say, "Psst, psst! I got the news, I got the news. Caine, blow, Beam me up, Scotty."[13]

Some officials decry a community apathy that shrugs off the deaths largely confined to minority children. Arne Duncan, the National Secretary of Education and former CEO of Chicago schools, says "all hell would break loose" if the killings occurred in one of Chicago's upscale enclaves. "If that happened to one of Chicago's wealthiest suburbs—and God forbid it ever did—if it was a child being shot dead every two weeks in Hinsdale or Winnetka or Barrington, do you think the status quo would remain? There's no way it would."[14] Yet other officials seem resigned to the violence, noting such violence against children is hardly limited to Chicago. In a statement that both rings with truth and illustrates the official pessimism that surrounds the issue, Chicago Mayor Richard Daley noted "It's all over, the same thing. You go to a large city or small city, it's all over America. It's not unique to one community or one city."[15]

The illegal drug market serves as the financial engine for organized gang activity. Criminal gang members associated with more than 20,000 identifiable street gangs dominate the wholesale and retail end of the drug market. Many of these gangs are affiliates of major national gang organizations and the NDIC lists over twenty gang organizations with significant influence on the US drug market. These range from urban-based gangs like the Latin Kings and Gangster Disciples to motorcycle gangs like the Hells Angels or the Vagos.

The growing influence of large gang organizations in drug trafficking comes at the expense of local independent dealers or the neighborhood based criminal groups which previously controlled the local drug market. Some of the larger gangs have begun purchasing large quantities of drugs directly from traffickers on the Mexican border, bypassing the wholesale operators in their own areas:

For example, members of the Chicago-based Latin Kings street gang who operate in Midland, Texas purchase cocaine from Mexican traffickers in south Texas for $16,000 to $18,000 per kilogram, compared with $25,000 to $35,000 per kilogram from wholesale traffickers in Chicago. With this savings, the gang undersells other local dealers who do not have the capacity to buy large wholesale quantities directly from Mexican DTOs in Mexico or along the Southwest Border.[16]

LAW ENFORCEMENT RESPONSES

Authorities have devised a variety of tactics designed to impede traffickers at every stage of the distribution network. At the cultivation level, governments have utilized tactics including crops substitution programs where farmers are provided financial incentives to grow crops other than drug products. In some instances, economic development programs, "aimed at developing legitimate economic opportunities," have been implemented.[17] Some governments including Bolivia and Peru, have taken more direct steps including spraying crops with herbicide and direct seizure of crops. The United States also targets eradication and enforcement efforts against domestic drug producers.

Efforts by governments around the world to crack down on drug cultivation have had mixed results. In the border areas adjoining Laos, Thailand and Burma, repressive governmental measures have clearly had an impact. This area, known as the Golden Triangle, led the world in illicit opium production from the 1970s into the 1990s. For a variety of reasons, regional governments began to crack down on opium production and were clearly successful in suppressing the opium cultivation. This success brought with it some of the "unintended consequences" previously referred to and questions about the sustainability of the decline. The impact of the cultivation suppression fell mainly on peasant farmers, leading some authorities to note that "hundreds of thousands of peasants have been impoverished" and that "crop eradication and strict implementation of bans on cultivation have aggravated violent conflicts."[18] One observer in Laos noted "Opium in Laos is not the big problem anymore in the sense of drug production; it is a problem because farmers can't grow it anymore."[19]

Violence Against Police

In the city of Juarez, Mexico, a place where drug violence has been particularly viral, there is a monument dedicated to police officers killed in the line of duty. In January of 2008, two lists were found taped to the monument. On the first list, under the heading of THOSE WHO DID NOT BELIEVE were the names of five recently murdered police officers. On the second list, under the heading FOR THOSE WHO CONTINUE NOT BELIEVING are the names of seventeen active police officers.[20] A few days later, four cops on the second list were killed. Forty cops have left the force since the first of the year...the police announced they would no longer be answering calls but preferred to stay in their station houses.[21]

Governments across the globe invest heavily in interdiction efforts to stop drug smuggling across their borders. These efforts are not limited to the large consumer nations of Europe and the United States. In fact, one of the most intense national efforts against traffickers likely belongs to the Iranian government which has spent $900 million on fences, towers and enforcement personnel to protect its borders with Afghanistan and Pakistan from drug smugglers.[22] "Smugglers are heavily armed, even occasionally using military tanks for these purposes."[23] These efforts have come with a heavy human cost as well, with Iran reporting that 250 border guards have died in recent years in combat with the traffickers.

Closer to home, Mexico has deployed increasing numbers of military to combat drug-related violence in border areas. With an escalating death toll reaching over 40,000 by 2011, the situation grows increasingly desperate.[24] The U.S. military, utilizing lessons learned fighting insurgency in Iraq and Afghanistan, is growing increasingly involved in training and advising the Mexican government in the fight against traffickers.[25]

Law enforcement interdiction efforts are not limited to cross-border smuggling. Drug routes from the initial point of entry in the United States generally follow the interstate highway system to large population centers, where they are rerouted to large and small jurisdictions across the country. Illegal drugs, like almost any other commodity, are transported via the country's highways. Police agencies, particularly state police who operate primarily along the roadways, interdict a percentage of the drugs enroute, often making large seizures. Despite the quantity of the seizure, truck drivers or other individuals actually in possession of the drugs are generally low-level workers with little or no knowledge of the trafficking operation. Traffickers make heavy use of these expendable individuals in all phases of the operation in order to insulate themselves from the risk of arrest.

Drug arrests reported in the media capture this phenomenon. In Ouachita Parish, Louisiana, a deputy stopped an 18-wheeler on I-20. The driver was nervous, unsure of his itinerary, and had a criminal history of drug offenses. The truck was carrying cucumbers but Lieutenant Stan Felts noticed an odor unlike any cucumbers he had ever smelled. A search discovered over 100 pounds of cocaine valued at $1.2 million. The driver, Salvador Gonzalez, was held on a two million dollar bond.[26]

In Tulsa, Oklahoma, Police Officer David Wansley investigated what appeared to be an abandoned pick-up. The truck was hauling an enclosed trailer and Wansley called a drug dog to the scene. The dog alerted and 1,500 pounds of marijuana were eventually discovered on a search of the trailer. No one was arrested.[27]

In the first story, despite the high bond and likely heavy prison sentence facing Mr. Gonzalez, the odds of him being a real player in the trafficking network are miniscule. Gonzalez was probably a low-level recruit promised a small lump sum for delivery of the truck. With the cocaine and cucumbers now in the hands of the authorities, the traffickers simply write the loss off as the cost of doing business. In the second instance, while 1,500 pounds of marijuana represents a nice hit for the police involved, the effects of this seizure in the illegal market will be negligible.

Law enforcement officials at all levels target high level dealers. In addition to the potential for major seizures of drug product and money, taking out high level dealers theoretically affects organizational leadership within the trafficking organization weakening their ability to effectively conduct their business. However, major dealers too often evade investigative efforts around large quantities of drugs. Rueter notes, "In the United states the federal government targets such dealers and now has about 100,000 persons incarcerated for drug offenses, the vast majority for some involvement in high level trafficking. However, many of those incarcerated for such offenses were convicted because they were caught with large quantities; their actual responsibilities may have been minor."[28]

Local drug enforcement varies widely across the country. Most major city police departments devote substantial resources from DARE officers to undercover operations and even in small jurisdictions, drug enforcement has become a routine fact of life. It would be difficult to find any police agency that would not identify drug problems as an issue for their department. Small jurisdictions often cooperate to field multi-agency units with each department providing officers and resources to a regional drug enforcement team.

The intensity and scope of enforcement activity varies tremendously. Local police departments target street markets, utilizing buy-bust and jump-out operations, drug sweeps and undercover drug purchases in the hope of disrupting and suppressing the street market. Every drug arrest presents the opportunity to turn the individual into an informant, hoping to move up the drug distribution chain to bigger traffickers. Once higher level dealers are identified, wire-taps, undercover infiltration into the organization and surveillance activities can effectively be utilized. The popular HBO television series, *The Wire*, was a realistic depiction of police drug suppression tactics.

Drug buyers in the street market can also be targeted. Sting operations, using undercover officers acting as street drug dealers, are an effective way of temporarily suppressing street sales at a particular location. The publicity accompanying such operations also serves as a warning to other drug buyers on the risk of the illegal market.

Communities around the country have also mobilized to fight back against street drug markets. A compilation of community-based strategies published by the Department of Justice includes:

> *Operating a telephone hotline*—Allows community members to anonymously and easily report drug dealing activity.
> *Encouraging place managers to be more proactive*—Many street markets exist adjacent to convenience store type operations. This strategy asks managers to actively discourage loitering and dealing in the vicinity of their business.

Applying nuisance abatement laws—This strategy compels property owners to take action to discourage drug dealing.
Notifying mortgage holders of drug-related problems at their properties—Negligent or absentee management creates an environment that allows drug markets to thrive.
Installing surveillance cameras—Together with effective publicity, the cameras can effectively move the drug market activity.
Altering access routes and restricting parking—Traffic *patterns* and parking restrictions can make it more difficult for buyers and sellers to maneuver in and out of the market.[29]

While getting drugs into the US is clearly the top priority of the traffickers, moving cash generated through the illegal market represents a difficult business challenge for them as well. A 2007 NDIC report estimates that at least $17.2 billion was smuggled into Mexico in 2003 and 2004. The moving of drug cash proceeds reverses the path of the drugs into the US:

Millions of dollars in bulk cash is transported each week from U.S. drug markets to relatively few consolidation areas such as Atlanta, Chicago, Los Angeles, New York City, and North Carolina, where a Mexican DTO bulk cash cell leader takes direct control of the money. These drug proceeds are subsequently shipped to or across the Southwest Border.[30]

DISCUSSION

Governmental authorities across the globe direct enormous resources geared to suppressing the illegal drug market. When combined with the bleak assessment that the impact on traffickers has been negligible, any rational citizen would begin to question current policies. The situation appears unlikely to improve in the near future. Drug related violence in Mexico continues to worsen. An estimated 40,000 people have been killed in drug-related violence since the Mexican government initiated a crackdown on drug cartels in 2007. Over 2800 deaths were recorded in the drug war in 2007, a figure that jumped to 9635 in 2009. The death toll for 2010 appears headed for even higher total with 3365 people killed during the first three months of the year.[31] While the border violence continues unabated, Mexican trafficking organizations have strengthened their stranglehold on many US drug markets, even in suburban and rural areas. The National Drug Intelligence Center notes "As a result, disrupting illicit drug availability and distribution will become increasingly difficult for state and local law enforcement agencies."[32]

Drug-related violence is described euphemistically by policy-makers as one of the "unintended consequences of prohibition."[33] Others of the unintended consequences listed include political instability in drug producing countries such as Columbia, where the rebel movement FARC has gained popular support by aligning itself with coca farmers victimized by government anti-drug programs.[34] International enforcement efforts have illustrated a "balloon effect" in the world drug market, which is "the ability of drug production to move to a new location within a country or across international borders, in response to events that reduce the attractiveness of existing production areas."[35]

The drug business also appears somewhat impervious to loses of product and money. A reduction in cocaine availability between 2006 and 2009 provides an example. A number of measures tracked the decline in the national supply of cocaine including workplace drug testing, emergency room admissions and reports from law enforcement officials across the country. Federal authorities offered several causes for the shortage including enforcement efforts at drug transit points and several large seizures of cocaine destined for the US via Mexico. Unfortunately, it appears that an expanding world market, particularly the "highly profitable market" of Europe may underlay the cocaine shortage in the US. Traffickers may be moving their product in response to higher profit potential in other places as opposed to successful suppression of the US market. It is also notable that as a cocaine shortage appeared, the availability of heroin, methamphetamine and cannabis all increased.[36]

Large seizures of illicit cash from traffickers also appear to have little effect on the illegal market. The NDIC report notes that cash couriers intercepted by authorities are instructed to deny knowledge of the cash, allowing law enforcement to seize the money. The dollar loss is apparently written off as a cost of business. The ability of the drug market to shrug off the large losses of product and cash is an indicator of the huge revenue and profits that accrue from the business.

In describing the efforts against the illegal drug market, the tendency is too both begin and end the discussion with law enforcement. While law enforcement is clearly the major player, other community efforts may also offer effective strategies. A new generation of drug prevention programs raises hopes that educational efforts to immunize Americans against serious drug involvement may be bearing fruit.

Drug treatment represents an underused and unrecognized strategy to combat the illegal drug market. A wealth of research documents the fact that on average "treatment reduces the extent of drug use and related health and social problems in those who enter programs."[37] Every addict in treatment or in continuing recovery represents a loss of income to the drug market.

Unfortunately, describing the workings of the drug market is easier than prescribing effective countermeasures The tremendous resources in both personnel and money directed at the illegal market together with the bleak assessment of these efforts as a failure suggests a change in policy direction. The nature and scope of such change is less clear. While the overall effort described as the "war on drugs" may fairly be termed a failure, there are pockets of success that policy-makers can build on. Building on these small successes will mean marginal improvement. Real impact on the problem will require bolder action.

BLUEPRINT FOR A NEW DIRECTION

A few key elements in the illegal drug market provide the cornerstones for a new direction. The first is noting the reality that the overwhelming bulk of the illegal drug business occurs on American street corners at the retail level. Reuter notes that 90% of the money and the personnel involved in the illegal drug market operate at the retail level.[36] This means that our ability to suppress the illegal market lies in our own hands. While it is easy to blame corrupt officials and foreign governments for the American drug problem, the fact is that the dollars handed to dealers by American users and addicts on street corners across the country are the financial engine for the corruption and violence from our city streets to the Mexican border.

The second reality is that marijuana is the primary product that supplies the revenue to the illegal market. If we are to effectively squeeze off the revenue that supports the illegal drug market, policy changes relating to marijuana will have to be addressed.

The third key element is the role that addicts play in the illegal market. Recognition that addicted people are the customer base that allows the market to thrive means that changing how we respond to addiction has the potential to divert these high volume customers away from the illegal market. Moving a substantial percentage of these buyers out of the market will effectively choke off revenue to the traffickers.

Both our own history of drug control efforts and a review of international efforts to suppress the drug market provide some important lessons as this new direction is developed. The ongoing movement toward the liberalization of marijuana policy in the country and its impact on the drug market also offers clues for policy changes.

Perhaps most importantly, insight into the dynamics of drug use and addiction and their major role in support of the illegal drug market offer real hope in steps to effectively take addicts out of the market.

NOTES

1. Reuter, Peter; Trautmann, Franz; Pacula, Rosalie Liccardo;, Kilmer, Beau; Gageldonk, Andre; van der Gouwe, Daan. (2009) "Assessing Changes in Global Drug Problems, 1998-2000." The Rand Corporation.
2. Ibid.
3. NDIC (2010). *National Drug Threat Assessment, 2010.* National Drug Intelligence Center, Department of Justice, Washington, D.C.
4. Ibid.
5. Conery, Ben. (2009) "Marijuana Found in Another National Park." *The Washington Times.* August 29, 2009. Retrieved from http://www.washingtontimes.com/news/2009/aug/29/.
6. Ibid.
7. NDIC, 2010.

8. Ibid.
9. Ibid.
10. Reuter, et al., 2009.
11. Harocopos, Alex and Hough, Mike. (2005) *Drug Dealing in Open-Air Markets.* Department of Justice, Office of Community Oriented Policing. Washington, D.C.
12. Mattingly, David. (2009, May8). "Minority Youngsters Dying Weekly on Chicago's Streets." Retrieved from http://www.cnn.com/2009/CRIME/05/08/chicago.children.slain.
13. Anderson, Elijah. (1999) *Code of the Streets: Decency, Violence, and the Moral Life of the Inner City.* W.W. Norton and Company, New York, N.Y, 29-30.
14. Mattingly, 2009.
15. Ibid.
16. NDIC, 2010, 12.
17. Reuter, et al., 2009.
18. Kramer, Tom; Jelsma, Martin; Blickman, Tom. (2009, January) *Withdrawal Symptoms in the Golden Triangle: A Drugs Market in Disarray.* Transnational Institute, Amsterdam, Netherlands. P. 25.
19. Ibid.
20. Bowden, Charles (2010). *Murder City.* Nation Books, New York, NY. P. 4.
21. Ibid, 5.
22. Reuter, et al., 2009.
23. Ibid, 40.
24. Castillo, E. Eduardo. (2010) "Gunmen Kill 15 Mexican Officers." Associated Press, June 15, 2010.
25. Michaels, Jim. "Mexican Military Gets US Advice." Cincinnati Enquirer. April 8, 2010, A6.
26. Hamilton, Matthew (2010). "18-Wheeler's Load Included Cucumbers, 105 Pounds of Cocaine." The News Star, April 14, 2010. Retrieved from http://www.thenewsstar.com/article/20100414.
27. Hampton, Deon and Adcock, Clifton (2010). "Police Seize 1,500 Pounds of Marijuana." Tulsa World, April 17, 2010. Retrieved from http://www.tulsaworld.com/news/.
28. Reuter, et al,. 2009, 41.
29. Harocopos and Hough, 2005.
30. NDIC, 2010, 47.
31. Castillo, 2010.
32. Reuter, et al, 2009, 47.
33. Ibid.
34. Ibid.
35. NDIC, 2010.
36. Reuter, et al, 2009, 37.

Chapter 3

Learning from the Past

> *"The final issue is not whether we will conquer drug abuse, but how soon."*
> *President Richard Nixon, 1971*

> *"We're going to win the war on drugs."*
> *President Ronald Reagan, 1982*

> *"This scourge will stop."*
> *President George H. Bush, 1989*

> *"President Bush hasn't fought a real war on crime and drugs. I will."*
> *President Bill Clinton, 1992*

In the early 1900s, heroin and cocaine were available at the corner drugstore. Heroin and other morphine derivatives were key ingredients in the patent medicines widely used in that era. (1) Hay fever remedies and the widely-popular drink Coca-Cola contained cocaine as an active ingredient. Cocaine was not only a trendy additive in wine, but also in cocoa-leaf cigarettes as well. Cocaine-laced "tablets, ointments, and sprays" were all available.[1] Heroin was popular as a tonic for a wide variety of ailments. A 1904 pharmacy ad claimed, "Heroin clears the complexion, gives buoyancy to the mind, regulates the stomach and bowels, and is, in fact, a perfect guardian of health."[2]

A variety of factors converged to turn the American populace against these drugs. Two key factors were the association of these drugs with repressed minorities and a growing recognition of the addiction problem. In 1900, America had an "addict population of 250,000" and an increasing "fear of addiction."[3]

Opium use was identified with Chinese immigrants and smoking opium was viewed as one of the tools with which "the Chinese were supposed to undermine American society."[4]

In the early 1900's, cocaine use was widely linked to African-Americans. Use of cocaine by African-Americans was believed to be a "spur to violence against whites."[5] It was popularly believed that cocaine use, particularly among blacks, caused super-human strength making "blacks almost unaffected by mere .32 caliber bullets."[6] Under this belief, a number of Southern police departments equipped officers with .38 caliber weapons.

The growing public antipathy towards opium and cocaine led to the Harrison Act of 1914 which became the legislative foundation for drug prohibition. As originally passed, the act was seen as "routine slap at a moral evil"[7] and it was somewhat overshadowed by the alcohol prohibition debate. At the time of the passage of the Harrison Act, there was little debate in the country over the dangers of opiates including heroin and cocaine. Musto notes that:

> By 1914, prominent newspapers, physicians, pharmacists, and congressmen believed opiates and cocaine predisposed habitués toward insanity and crime. They were widely seen as substances associated with foreigners or alien subgroups. Cocaine raised the specter of the wild Negro, opium the devious Chinese, morphine the tramps in the slums.[8]

Marijuana took a somewhat different path to prohibition. Although inclusion of marijuana under the Harrison Act was considered, it was eventually excluded, largely as a result of opposition by the pharmaceutical industry. In the early 1900s leading up to the Harrison Act, not even those pushing for the Harrison Act believed that "cannabis was a problem of any major significance in the United States."[9] However, in the years following passage of the Harrison Act, alleged violence associated with marijuana use by Mexican immigrants became the catalyst for prohibition legislation. By the middle of the 1920s, marijuana was increasingly perceived as the cause of extreme violence among Mexicans. "By the mid-twenties horrible crimes were attributed to marijuana and its Mexican purveyors. Legal and medical officers in New Orleans began studies of the evil and within a few years published articles claiming that many of the region's crimes could be traced to marihuana, for they believed it was a sexual stimulant that removed civilized inhibitions."[10]

By 1937, concern about marijuana resulted in the passage of the Marijuana Tax Act. Using the tax code as a prohibition mechanism was a legislative tactic which had been used in 1934 to prohibit machine guns. The bill had little opposition with only AMA spokesman William Woodward testifying against it. Woodward believed the evidence against marihuana was incomplete, an unpopular stance. Woodward was "bombarded with hostile questions" and following brief hearings, the bill passed.[11] Successful passage of the Marijuana Tax Act opened the door to a flood of marijuana prohibition legislation at every governmental level.

From the "Noble Experiment," as Alcohol Prohibition was described by President Herbert Hoover, to the various "Wars on Drugs," there has been no shortage of attempts to control America's drug problem. The results of these various efforts have been mixed, with some notable successes. The broad campaign against tobacco is one clear success as American smoking rates have dropped dramatically over the last fifty years. Likewise, the movement to reduce drunken driving has clearly achieved significant goals. A review of past efforts such as these can provide some guidance in seeking more effective approaches to our drug problems.

ALCOHOL PROHIBITION

On passage of the 18th amendment to the US Constitution, prohibitionist Billy Sunday exclaimed, "The reign of tears is over. The slums will soon be a memory. We will turn our prisons into factories...Hell will be for rent."[12] While not quite as enthusiastic as Reverend Sunday, many Americans of the time supported prohibition.

Alcohol has always been a significant part of American society. In fact, in packing for their trip to the new world, our ancestors on the Mayflower brought more beer than water on board.[13] In Colonial America, hard-drinking was common. American per capita consumption in 1790 was approximately six gallons of 200 proof alcohol, an amount nearly double the current consumption rate and nearly triple the per capita consumption rate in the decade just prior to prohibition.[14]

Temperance sentiment also has a long-standing history in America. While there is little evidence of concern about alcohol in Colonial times, in the early nineteenth century, the Temperance movement began to assert itself. Historian Jack Larkin noted that "the American way of drunkenness began to lose ground as early as the mid 1820's."[15]

In 1851, Maine became the first state to legally ban alcohol and over the next 60 years several states followed. Many of the bans passed by these states were riddled with loopholes. Many of them allowed mail order delivery of alcohol and prohibited only hard liquor. A key legislative step in the movement toward prohibition was the War Prohibition Act of 1918, which defined intoxicating beverages prohibited as those containing more than 2.75% alcohol content. This allowed people to continue to legally consume light beer and wine, a practice also allowed under a number of the previously passed state prohibition laws.[16]

The 18th Amendment dictating national prohibition was ratified in 1919 and Congress passed the Volstead Act, implementing prohibition, on October 28,

1919. The Volstead Act took many Americans by surprise when it did not follow the War Prohibition Act definition of prohibited alcohol but instead set the prohibition threshold at one-half of one percent alcohol content. This had the practical effect of banning not only hard liquor, but wine and beer as well, a shock to the executives in the beer and wine industry, many of whom had supported prohibition believing their form of alcoholic beverage would be allowed.[17]

A significant percentage of Americans did not support the stringent standards imposed by the Volstead Act. A 1922 poll found 40% of citizens believed light beer and wine should be allowed under prohibition. The same poll found 62% of Americans favoring lenient enforcement of the Volstead Act. In extending the reach of prohibition beyond that supported by many Americans, the advocates of prohibition likely sowed the seeds of eventual repeal.[18]

The imposition of Prohibition also had a devastating economic impact. Blocker notes that only rarely had the federal government acted in a fashion to shut down an entire industry:

> In 1916, there were 1300 breweries producing full-strength beer in the United States; 10 years later there were none. Over the same period, the number of distilleries was cut by 85%, and most of the survivors produced little but industrial alcohol. Legal production of near beer used less than one tenth the amount of malt, one twelfth the rice and hops, and one thirtieth the corn used to make full-strength beer before National Prohibition. The 318 wineries of 1914 became the 27 of 1925. The number of liquor wholesalers was cut by 96% and the number of legal retailers by 90%.[19]

While many companies simply shut their doors and went out of business, others adapted. The Coors Brewing Company, Miller, and Anheuser-Busch all moved to production of near-beer, porcelain products, and malted milk.[20] Prohibition banned not only manufacture of alcohol, but importation and transportation as well. As a result of these actions, the legal distribution network was eliminated, creating a vacuum soon filled largely by organized crime.

Whatever their misgivings, in the early years of Prohibition, Americans followed the law. While exact figures on alcohol consumption during Prohibition do not exist, it is clear that Prohibition had an impact. Zimring and Hawkins note that the death rate from cirrhosis declined from 29.5 per 100,000 in 1911 to 10.7 per 100,000 in 1929:

> Admissions to state mental hospitals for disease classified as alcoholic psychosis fell from 10.1 in 1919, to 3.7 in 1922...National records for arrests for drunkenness and disorderly conduct declined 50% between 1916 and 1922. Reports from welfare agencies around the country overwhelmingly indicated a dramatic decrease among client population of alcohol-related family problems.[21]

While the public health results from prohibition appear positive, prohibition's crime impact was stunning. Writer Gore Vidal captured the popular view of prohibition when he claimed Prohibition had led to "the greatest crime wave in the country's history."[22]

The criminal violence following prohibition was most striking in Chicago, where notorious gangster Al Capone waged a brutal war to gain total control of the illegal alcohol business. Historian Andrew Sinclair noted that Capone's competitors in the illegal alcohol business "fled for their lives. In the time of the consolidation of Capone's power in Chicago, there were between 350-400 murders annually in Cook County, Illinois and an average of 100 bombings each year."[23]

The profits connected with illegal bootlegging were enormous. Sinclair wrote, "In its practical effects, national prohibition transferred two billion dollars a year from the hands of brewers, distillers and shareholders to the hands of murderers, crooks and illiterates...Capone was making between $60,000,000 and $100,000,000 a year from the sale of beer alone."[24]

The Wickersham Commission, a federal study group reviewing the results of the National Prohibition Act, stated that illegal proceeds from bootlegging "offers rewards on a par with the most important legitimate industries. It makes lavish expenditures in corruption possible. It affords a financial basis for organized crime."[25] By 1931, the Commission described the state of enforcement of prohibition as "appalling" and "growing steadily worse."[26]

The Commission also noted the eroding public support of prohibition. It reported "adverse public opinion in some states and lukewarm public opinion with hostile elements in some states [presented] a serious obstacle to the observance and enforcement of the national prohibition laws."[27]

In fact, a significant percentage of the public was openly antagonistic to prohibition and illegal drinking flourished. By 1925, in New York City alone, "there were anywhere between 30,000 to 100,000 speakeasy clubs. The demand for alcohol was outweighing (and out-winning) the demand for sobriety. People found clever ways to evade Prohibition agents. They carried hip flasks, hollowed canes, false books, and the like."[28]

The final straw for an American public growing increasingly hostile to the temperance movement was passage of the Jones Act in March of 1929. Named after its legislative sponsor, Senator Wesley Jones of Washington, the law upped the criminal penalties for violation of the Volstead Act for first time offenders to a five year jail sentence and a $10,000 fine.[29]

Dubbed the "Jones 5 and 10 law," resulting enforcement quickly clogged the courts and jails with small time violators. Public outrage at the law and at Jones exploded. "The protest that followed [the Jones Act] was immediate, national, bitter and abusive. Senator Jones found himself attacked without mercy in newspapers, in state legislatures, in Congress, even in the federal court."[30]

In 1930, as an indicator of the deep public antipathy toward prohibition, the Pabst Brewing Company invested a million dollars in the modernization of their facilities in anticipation of the end of prohibition.[31] By 1932, prohibition was a major issue in the presidential campaign with the "Dry" candidate Herbert Hoover opposed by Franklin Roosevelt, a strong supporter of prohibition repeal.

In 1932, in the midst of the Great Depression, the argument for repeal also centered on economic recovery. "Repeal, it was argued, would replace the tax revenues foregone under Prohibition, thereby allowing governments to provide relief to suffering families. It would put unemployed workers back to work."[32]

The majority of observers describe National Prohibition as a failure, noting simply that the 18th Amendment is the only constitutional amendment repealed in the history of the republic. A few disagree. Focusing primarily on the public health benefits of prohibition, J.C. Burham writes that "until sometime in the 1920's...when enforcement had clearly broken down, prohibition was generally a success."[33]

Yet prohibition was likely doomed from the start. Andrew Sinclair eloquently captures the challenge. "Alcohol is easy to make, simple to sell, pleasant to consume and few men will refuse so facile a method of escaping from the miseries of living."[34]

In judging the prohibition experiment, it is hard to disagree with John Kaplans's verdict "that our experience between 1920 and 1933 ...demonstrated that as bad as a drug might be, there could be laws that were worse."[35]

THE FIGHT AGAINST TOBACCO

Tobacco has been used by humans for nearly 6000 years.[36] While some of our ancient ancestors undoubtedly detested tobacco use, the first known public smoking ban was issued by Pope Urban VII in 1590 when he threatened to excommunicate anyone who "took tobacco in the porchway of or inside a church, whether it be by chewing it, smoking it with a pipe or sniffing it...through the nose."[37]

Adolf Hitler was a rabid anti-smoker and Nazi Germany organized the first anti-smoking campaign in modern history. The Nazi campaign included smoking bans on public transportation, punitive cigarette taxes, and restrictions on tobacco advertising.[38]

In the United States, the Surgeon General's report of 1964 highlighting the health dangers of smoking was a watershed moment in the movement against tobacco. In the early 1960's, smoking was common. Over fifty percent of men and over thirty-five percent of women smoked. In 1961, a coalition of health agencies including both the American Cancer Society and the American Heart Association requested that a study group be appointed "to consider the responsibilities of government, of business and of voluntary agencies relative to the health hazards of cigarette smoking and to recommend a solution of this health problem that would protect the public and would interfere least with the freedom of industry and the happiness of individuals."[39]

In response to this request, in 1962, Surgeon General Doctor Luther Terry announced the formation of an expert committee to review data on smoking and health. The committee consisted of carefully chosen scientists, all of whom were deemed neutral on the smoking issue. All members of the committee were jointly screened by tobacco industry representatives and the American Medical Association. By agreement, fifty percent of those appointed to the committee were smokers.

On January 11, 1964, the Committee released its report. In over 15 months of study, the Committee had reviewed over 400 research reports and interviewed over 150 research investigators. The end result was "the most comprehensive and authoritative report on this subject ever made."[40]

The report was daunting in its indictment of smoking as a health hazard. On lung cancer, the report noted that smoking was "causally related" and further, "the magnitude of the effect of cigarette smoking far outweighs other factors."[41] With reference to coronary disease, the report stated, "Male cigarette smokers have a higher death rate from coronary artery disease than non-smoking males, but it is not clear that the association has causal significance."[42] However, the evidence was substantial enough that the Committee noted "It is more prudent to assume the established association...has causative meaning than to suspend judgment until no uncertainty remains."[43]

The Surgeon General's report caught the attention of the public as well as government officials. Fifteen billion fewer cigarettes were sold in 1964 than 1963, a decline of just over 2%. Yet this was the first decline in a pattern of cigarette consumption that had increased over 200 fold between 1900 and 1960. Per capita cigarette consumption had more than doubled in the 20 years between 1940 and 1960. The consumption drop in 1964 was credited to publicity surrounding the Surgeon General's Report.[44]

The Report was the impetus for an escalating series of governmental steps against tobacco. In June of 1964, the Federal Trade Commission (FTC) ruled that cigarette advertising was deceptive and proposed that information on tar and nicotine content as well as warning labels be affixed to cigarette packs to make smokers aware of the health risks. The FTC proposed label read: "Caution: Cigarette Smoking is Dangerous to Health. It May Cause Death from Cancer and Other Diseases."[45]

The tobacco industry responded with a lobbying effort that emasculated the FTC proposals. The Cigarette Labeling and Advertising Act ultimately passed by Congress was described by the New York Times as "a shocking piece of special-interest legislation—a bill to protect the economic health of the tobacco industry by freeing it of proper regulation."[46]

The warning label approved by the Congress read "Cigarette smoking may be hazardous to your health."[47] The legislation also mandated a study of the effectiveness of the warning label and the required study was completed in 1969. After review of the research, the FTC study concluded "There is virtually no evidence that the warning statement on cigarette packages has had any significant effect."[48]

The small drop in cigarette consumption following the Surgeon General's Report in 1964 was reversed the next year and consumption increased again until 1969. The decrease in 1969 was attributed to the results of both tobacco tax increases and advertising changes. Between 1965 and 1969 cigarette consumption increased 3.5% but in 1969 it dropped 2.5% in a single year.[49]

There were significant state tobacco tax increases immediately prior to 1969 which probably contributed to the reduction in sales during that year. During fiscal year 1967, fifteen states increased their cigarette tax rates; the average increase was 3.5 cents per pack. The rate increases ranged from New York's, Ohio's, and Illinois's two cents per pack to California's and Florida's seven cents per pack. The next year, seven more states increased their cigarette taxes. The rates ranged from Massachusetts's and Vermont's two cents per pack to Minnesota's, Rhode Island's, and Tennessee's five cents per pack while the average increase was approximately four cents per pack.[50]

> **Drugs and Guns Killing New York**
>
> A Bronx double homicide last month typified the city's drug killings. Saleem Sterling, who had been arrested three times for possession, was shot to death with a second man outside a building in the Soundview Houses. Sterling, 30, had drugs stashed inside a body cavity, police said.[51]

By 1969, the shift in public opinion against tobacco was in full swing. In 1968, the Federal Communications Commission (FTC) ruled that under the Fairness Doctrine, radio and TV stations were required to provide counter advertising to tobacco advertising. By 1971 a total ban on cigarette advertising on television and radio was in effect. In a concession to broadcasters concerned with loss of advertising revenue, the ban was delayed for one day to allow cigarette advertising to appear on broadcasts on the New Year's Day football bowl games. The estimated loss to television and radio stations stemming from the ban amounted to $220 million per year, just under eight percent of their total revenue.[52]

Increasing cigarette taxes has become a popular tactic for both raising government revenue and discouraging smoking. Since 2002, states have increased their cigarette taxes more than eighty times. The state of New York now claims the highest cigarette tax rate in the country at $2.75 per pack. The average state rate is $1.19 per pack. Adding in the federal tax rate of $.39 per pack puts the tax burden of an average pack of cigarettes at about $1.50 per pack.[53]

Justifying tax increases on cigarettes is relatively easy given the volume of statistics linking smoking with a long list of health problems. The health care costs related to smoking are huge by any measure. Pinning down exact smoking related costs is difficult. The Centers for Disease Control (CDC) peg the health care related costs of smoking at $10.28 per pack.[54] Other studies put the health related costs as high as $33 per pack and adding in costs associated with second hand smoke runs the estimated total cost to nearly $40 per pack.[55]

The current debate over raising cigarette taxes in the state of Kentucky illustrates the issue. With an adult smoking rate of 28.2%, Kentucky has the highest incidence of smoking among all the states.[56] As one of the major tobacco producing states, Kentucky has historically been a state hostile to tobacco taxes, currently ranking 47th among the states in tobacco tax rate.[57]

The change in the climate toward cigarette taxes in Kentucky is a vivid example of the sea-change in community attitudes toward tobacco. The Kentucky Chamber of Commerce, a business group which generally views corporate taxes with the same enthusiasm one might generate for an upcoming root canal, supported the 2009 effort to increase the tobacco tax. The reason for the change is the awareness of the health-related economic effects of smoking. Mike Ridenour, Chamber spokesperson, noted that when members saw estimates on the cost of smoking, "they were stunned."[58]

Economists believe tax increases are an efficient way to decrease smoking. Advocates claim the imposition of the proposed $.70 per pack tax in Kentucky would reduce both youth and adult smoking. But the biggest savings would be in long term health related expenses and the tax itself would generate an estimated $200 million annually for the state treasury.[59]

Governmental action against tobacco has been supplemented by private sector initiatives. Corporate action to deter tobacco has moved beyond restrictions on smoking in the workplace to a direct targeting of smoking behavior. Parekh notes that "Thirty-two percent [of corporations] offer a smoking cessation program; 27% have policies limiting the number of breaks employees can take during the day; 17% have written policies stating that smoking in undesignated areas may result in termination; 5% charge higher health care premiums for smokers; and 2% ask about smoking behavior in the recruiting process."[60]

Meanwhile, increased government regulation of smoking is showing no signs of a slowdown. In December of 2008, Boston officials followed San Francisco authorities in approving a ban on tobacco sales in pharmacies. Boston went further than San Francisco when it barred smoking on college campuses as well as smoking restrictions on a variety of businesses including loading docks.[61] These regulations may have some impact locally, but federal legislation passed in 2009 has the potential to dramatically escalate government regulation of tobacco products.

On June 22, 2009 President Obama signed into law the Family Smoking Prevention and Tobacco Control Act which authorizes the U.S. Food and Drug Administration (FDA) to regulate tobacco products for the first time. The legislation contains sweeping new restrictions on tobacco products. The new law will

- Crack down on tobacco marketing and sales to kids.
- Ban candy and fruit-flavored cigarettes.
- Require larger, more effective health warnings on tobacco products.
- Require tobacco companies to disclose the contents of tobacco products, as well as changes in products and research about their health effects.

- Ban terms such as "light" and "low-tar" that mislead consumers into believing that certain cigarettes are safer.
- Strictly regulate all health-related claims about tobacco products to ensure they are scientifically proven and do not discourage current tobacco users from quitting or encourage new users to start.
- Empower the FDA authority to require changes in tobacco products, such as the removal or reduction of harmful ingredients.[62]

This legislation, taking effect in June of 2010, imposes a variety of new regulations on nearly every aspect of the tobacco business, from the manufacture of cigarettes, to advertising, to packaging restrictions, to limits on the use of free samples.

THE FIGHT AGAINST DRUNK DRIVING

Efforts to control drunk driving date nearly to the beginnings of the automotive age. A 1904 study of twenty-five (25) fatal automobile accidents found nineteen (19) of the drivers had used "spirits" within one hour prior to the accident.[63] In New York, the first law banning drunk driving was passed in 1910, and other states soon followed suit.[64] These early laws did not set any standards for driving under the influence but relied on the judgment of the police officer to determine if the driver was impaired.

By the 1930's, with some improved technology, a Blood Alcohol Content (BAC) of .15% was set as the alcohol level that defined drunken driving. This level was chosen based on research by the American Medical Association and the National Safety Council.[65] BAC is determined not only by the amount of alcohol consumed, but the sex of the individual, their body composition and the drinking time period. Body weight is the most important of these, as larger people will have a lower BAC compared to a smaller person drinking the same amount. Sex is also a factor, with women reaching a somewhat higher BAC as an identically sized male drinking the same amount of alcohol.

To put the BAC level of .15 in context, consider that a 170 pound male would need to consume nine twelve ounce beers in a two hour period to reach this level. A 120 pound female would need to consume five twelve ounce beers in the same time period to reach the .15 threshold.[66]

Through the 1960s and 1970s, over 50,000 people each year were killed in traffic crashes. Between fifty and sixty percent of these were alcohol related.[67] Driving under the influence was widely accepted and there was evidence that even the 50% estimate of alcohol related traffic deaths was too conservative. A three year study in South Carolina found 67% of traffic fatalities including pedestrian deaths had BACs in excess of the legal limit. Roadside surveys across the country found rates of drunk driving at nearly 30% of drivers during weekend late night hours.[68]

In response, during the period of 1966 to 1977, the federal government funded Alcohol Safety Action Projects (ASAP) in 35 different cities. These efforts were designed to be comprehensive including police, courts, and social services in a coordinated fashion. The ASAP in Cincinnati typified the effort. Funding was provided to law enforcement to increase DUI arrests, a special court probation unit handling DUI cases was created, and a social service network to identify and treat those offenders diagnosed as alcoholic were all part of the project.

While traffic deaths declined in only 12 of the 35 sites, some of the successful programs made significant headway. In Cincinnati, traffic deaths in the year prior to the project (1971) totaled 88. City DUI arrests that same year totaled 460. With the support of project funding, Cincinnati Police dramatically increased DUI arrests, which jumped to 2906 in 1972, 3532 in 1973 and 3742 in 1974. Traffic deaths over the same period went from 88 to 63. In the years following, arrests remained at a level approximately four times the pre-project numbers and fatalities continued to decline reaching a low of 50 in 1978.[69]

In 1980, a drunk driving incident became the catalyst that would change American attitudes. On May 3 of that year, thirteen-year-old Cari Lightner was walking with a friend to a neighborhood festival near her home in Fair Oaks, California. Cari had just finished playing a morning softball game and was still in her uniform as she walked in the bicycle lane next to the roadway.

At a nearby bar, a man named Clarence William Busch had spent his morning finishing what would be a three day drinking binge. Busch was 47 years old, had three previous drunk driving convictions, and was out on bail after a hit-run, drunk driving episode only days earlier.

Barreling down the quiet residential street at high speed, Busch struck Cari from behind, throwing her 125 feet. Busch then sped off but was later apprehended by the police. In the midst of mourning for their daughter, Cari's parents were shocked to learn Busch's history and what they viewed as the cavalier attitude of the criminal justice system toward drunk driving.

Candi Lightner, Cari's mother, refused to accept the status quo and formed a victims' organization, Mothers Against Drunk Drivers (MADD). The Lightner's experience resonated with victims across the nation and MADD chapters began to spring up around the country. MADD quickly became a powerful force demanding reform of DUI laws.

MADD members began sitting in courtrooms around the country, recording the sentences handed down on DUI cases. They organized meetings with state legislators, demanding tougher penalties and mandatory jail time for DUI offenders. But perhaps their most powerful tool was personalizing the victims of drunk driving, thus demanding accountability for a crime in which victims had previously been nearly invisible.

MADD's advocacy is largely responsible for many of changes in the handling of DUI offenses. DUI offenses, once routinely plea-bargained, are treated much more harshly. Convictions bring mandatory incarceration in many cases and repeat offenses may bring significant jail time.

MADD pushed the .08 BAC level as the legal threshold for defining the offense of drunk driving and the .08 limit is now the law in every state in the country. The push to increase the national drinking age from 18 to 21 was spearheaded by MADD which also advocated for voluntary efforts now commonplace about the country such as the "designated driver" and "server liability training" programs.

The effort to reduce the carnage linked to drunk driving has been clearly successful and deaths from alcohol-related incidents have declined dramatically. In 1982, according to the National Highway Traffic Safety Administration (NHSTA), 26,173 Americans lost their lives in alcohol-related accidents. In 2007, the lives lost in alcohol-related accidents totaled 16,885, a reduction of 35%. This reduction occurred even as large increases were recorded in both the number of vehicles and the miles driven on American roadways.

DISCUSSION

The common thread that links the lessons of prohibition with the more recent efforts on tobacco and drunk driving is the role played by public support or non-support. Prohibition was crippled at the outset by a gap between the public expectation of what prohibition would entail and the reality of prohibition. The Volstead Act forced a prohibition more drastic than many Americans anticipated and their support evaporated with the imposition of a harsh prohibition regime. Further, many supporters of prohibition were not themselves abstainers but were those who, as Blocker noted, "believed that it was a good idea to control someone else's drinking (perhaps everyone else's), but not their own."[70]

Escalating crime and the government response to it also was a major contributor to the death of prohibition. In a somewhat eerie echo of today's drug policy debate, the 1929 Jones "5 and 10 act" imposed five-year jail sentences and $10,000 fines on first offenders who violated federal prohibition laws. The act struck many Americans as overly harsh and punitive, and enforcement of the Jones Act immediately flooded the jails with minor offenders. The primary sponsor of the act, Senator Wesley Jones of Washington, became the object of ridicule and outrage by a public growing hostile to the heavy hand of the temperance movement.[71]

As the prohibition era progressed, public perception of the temperance movement also shifted dramatically. As the movement toward prohibition gained momentum, it was viewed as a part of a larger progressive movement focused on improvements in health and welfare. However, as America moved into the 1920's, the view of prohibition as aligned with the progressive movement took a radical turn.

Inspired and led by the talented writers of the Lost Generation, the shapers of mass culture—first in novels, then in films, and finally in newspapers and magazines—altered the popular media's previously negative attitude toward drinking. In the eyes of many young people, especially the increasing numbers who populated colleges and universities, Prohibition was transformed from a progressive reform to an emblem of a suffocating status quo.[72]

Economic circumstances also played a role in changing public attitudes. In the early 1930s, mired in the Great Depression and with joblessness at record levels, the argument that ending prohibition would provide government funding for the array of public works proposed by the Roosevelt administration was persuasive.

The success in reducing tobacco consumption is also a tale of changing public attitudes. In the face of today's attitudes toward smoking, it is easy to forget that in the 1960s, over half of all men and over a third of women smoked. Smoking and other tobacco use was integrated into almost every activity—ashtrays were common in homes, restaurants, nightclubs and offices. Television talk show hosts like Johnny Carson smoked while interviewing guests and President Lyndon Johnson conducted press conferences with a cigarette in his hand.

Unlike the alcohol prohibition movement, the struggle against tobacco occurred within a legal and regulatory context. It was driven, first and foremost, by health concerns, thus avoiding the moralistic nature of the prohibition debate. In 1969, when the Federal Trade Commission ruled that, under the Fairness Doctrine, media would be required to broadcast anti-tobacco ads, tobacco advertising lost its dominance in the public debate. Two years later, tobacco advertising on television was banned, making it much more difficult for the tobacco industry to contest the increasing flood of anti-tobacco information disseminated by health agencies.

Increasing tobacco taxes was also a crucial factor in the success. Evidence that price increases were an effective method of suppressing demand, combined with the governmental hunger for revenue, has meant an ever increasing expense for tobacco users. Portraying tobacco taxes as a partial remedy for escalating health costs has also proved effective in building public and legislative support for these taxes.

The shift in the cultural mindset toward tobacco is both the fuel for and the result of changing public attitudes. Within the space of a single lifetime, the social view of tobacco use, particularly smoking, has been turned completely around. Smoking has gone from a behavior which was viewed as not only acceptable, but socially desirable, to a behavior which has become socially repugnant, making smokers outcasts among the larger community.

The battle to reduce drunken driving was very different from both the fight against tobacco and alcohol prohibition. Prohibition criminalized alcohol consumption targeting all users. The tobacco effort targeted all users, but within a regulatory context. The strategies of advertising controls, increasing taxes and restricting smoking to limited public places all combined to make tobacco use an inconvenient, expensive and socially stigmatized behavior. Effective public education on the health risks of smoking and the dangers of second-hand smoke have also played a crucial role.

In contrast, MADD and other advocates did not target alcohol use but instead one specific alcohol-related behavior, drunk driving. By narrowing the focus to a significant problem which put the public at risk, and speaking on behalf of victims, MADD marginalized most of the opposition to their proposals. The criminal justice handling of drunk driving was an area ripe for reform and by framing drunken driving as a violent crime and personalizing the victims, MADD created a demand for change public officials could not ignore.

This history illustrates at least one clear lesson—effective public support of drug laws will act to reinforce the law's intent, multiplying its effectiveness. Non-support will marginalize the law's intent, rendering it ineffective and potentially counter-productive.

Drug policy options cover a complex range of responses. An overview of policy choices as well as a framework to evaluate these choices is a crucial element in setting a new direction.

*For an excellent and detailed description of early American attempts to control drugs, see David Musto's *The American Disease*, Oxford University Press, 1987.

NOTES

1. Musto, David (1987). The American Disease, Oxford University Press, New York, NY., 7.
2. Kittrels, Alonzo (2006, November 27). "We've made amazing progress in the last century." Retrieved from http/www.gamehavoc.com/showthread.php?17247
3. Musto, David (1987). The American Disease, Oxford University Press, New York, NY., 5.
4. Ibid, 6.
5. Ibid, 7.
6. Ibid, 7.
7. Ibid, 65.
8. Ibid, 65.
9. Ibid, 217.
10. Ibid, 219.
11. Ibid, 227.
12. Engleman, Larry. (1979). *Intemperance: The Lost War Against Liquor.* New York, NY: Free Press, XI
13. Winkelman, R., Cannon, T. & Powell, J. *Alcohol Biology 105.* Retrieved from Lecture Notes Online Web site: http//www.mc.edu.campus/users/rhamilto/BIO1105/Alcoholppt.
14. Lender, M.E. & Martin, James K. (1987). *Drinking in America: A History.* New York, NY: Free Press, 205.
15. Larkin, Jack (1988). *The reshaping of everyday life, 1790-1840.* New York, NY: Harper & Row, 295.

16. Rickard, E. (2001, July 1). *How Dry We Were: The Repeal of Prohibition*. Retrieved from http://www.november.org/Prohibition/.
17. Ibid.
18. Ibid.
19. Blocker, J. (2006, February). "Did Prohibition Really Work? Alcohol Prohibition as a Public Health Innovation." *American Journal of Public Health*, 96(2): 239–241.
20. Ibid.
21. Zimring, F. & Hawkins, G. (1992). *The Search for Rational Drug Control*. New York, NY: Cambridge University Press: 63-64.
22. Vidal, G. (1972). *Homage to Daniel Shays: Collected essays 1952-1972*. New York, NY: Random House, 374.
23. Sinclair, A. (1964). *Era of Excess: A Social History of the Prohibition Movement*. New York, NY: Harper and Row, 222.
24. Ibid, 229.
25. National Commission on Law Observance and Enforcement. (1931, January 7). *Report on the Enforcement of the Prohibition Laws of the United States*. Washington D.C.: U.S. Government Printing Office.
26. Ibid, 108.
27. Ibid, 49.
28. Teaching with Documents: The Volstead Act. (2009) Retrieved from http://www.historicaldocuments.com/VolsteadAct.htm.
29. Lender and Martin, 1987.
30. Clark, N. H. (1976). *Deliver Us From Evil: An Interpretation of American Prohibition*. New York, NY: Norton Publishing, 195.
31. Lender and Martin, (1987). *Drinking in America: A history*. New York, NY: Free Press.
32. Blocker J. (2006, February). "Did prohibition really work? Alcohol prohibition as a public health innovation." *American Journal of Public Health*, 96(2), 247.
33. Burham, J.C. (1968). "Was Prohibition a Failure?" *Journal of Social History*, 1968-1969, 57.
34. Sinclair, A. (1964). *Era of excess: A social history of the prohibition movement*. New York, NY; Harper and Row, 415.
35. Zimring F. & Hawkins, G. (1992). *The Search for rational drug control*. New York, NY; Cambridge University Press, 69.
36. Tierra, M. (2007, June). *Brief History and Culture of Tobacco*. Retrieved from http://www.planetherbs.com/theory/brief-history-and-culture-of-tobacco.html.
37. "Anti-Smoking Movement." (2011) Retrieved from: http://en.wikipedia.org/wiki/Anti-tobaccomovementinnazigermany.
38. Proctor, R.N. (1997). "The Nazi War on Tobacco: Ideology, Evidence, and Possible Cancer Consequences." Bull Hist Med, 71(3): 435–88.
39. Diehl, H. (1969). *Tobacco and Your Health*. New York, NY: McGraw Hill Book Co, 155.
40. Ibid, 156.
41. Surgeon General's Advisory Committee on Smoking and Health. (1964). "Smoking and Health." Public Health Service Publication No. 1103. United States: Public Health Service. Office of the Surgeon General, 196.
42. Ibid, 327.
43. Ibid, 327.

44. McGrew, J. (2008). *History of Tobacco Regulation.* National Commission on Marihuana and Drug Abuse. Retrieved from http://www.druglibrary.org/Schaffer/LIBRARY/studies/nc/nc2b.htm.
45. Ibid.
46. Ibid.
47. Ibid.
48. Ibid.
49. "Cigarette Consumption, United States, 1900-2007." Retrieved from http://www.infoplease.com/ipa/A0908700.html
50. "Federal and State Cigarette Excise Taxes – United States, 1995-2009," MMWR Weekly (May 22, 2009), Center for Disease Control, Retrieved from http://www.cdc.gov/mmwr/preview/mmwrhtml/mm5819a2.htm
51. Sandoval, E., Parascandola, R. and McShane, L. (2010, December 2) "Drugs and guns are killing New York—two-thirds of murder victims are black, drugs involved." N.Y Daily News. Retrieved from http://articles.nydailynews.com/2010-12-02/news/27082935_1_murder-victims-drug-killings-murder-rate/2.
52. Wagner, S. (1971). *Cigarette Country.* New York, NY: Praeger Publishers.
53. "Federal and State Cigarette Excise Taxes – United States, 1995-2009," MMWR Weekly (May 22, 2009), Center for Disease Control, Retrieved from http://www.cdc.gov/mmwr/preview/mmwrhtml/mm5819a2.htm.
54. Ibid.
55. "Smoking's Real Cost Reaches $40 Per Pack Over Lifetime, Duke Study Concludes." Duke Today, November 22, 2004. Retrieved from http://today.duke.edu/2004/11/costofsmoking_1104.html
56. Vos, S. (2008, September 5). "Putting a Price on Smoking." *The Herald-Leader.* Retrieved from http://www.kentucky.com/181/story/514712.html.
57. "Federal and State Cigarette Excise Taxes – United States, 1995-2009," MMWR Weekly (May 22, 2009), Center for Disease Control, Retrieved from http://www.cdc.gov/mmwr/preview/mmwrhtml/mm5819a2.htm
58. Vos, S. (2008, September 5). "Putting a Price on Smoking." *The Herald-Leader.* Retrieved from http://www.kentucky.com/181/story/514712.html.
59. Ibid.
60. Parekh, R. (2005, February 28). "Companies fight tobacco use to lower health care costs." Business Insurance, 39(9), 4-5.
61. Rabinowitz, N. (2008). "Boston Commission Votes to Ban Cigar and Hookah bars, End Tobacco Sale on College Campuses." *Associated Press.* Retrieved from http://www.chicagotribune.com/news/nationworld/sns-ap-smoking-bar-ban9b,0,1404279.
62. Federal Drug Administration (2012). "Overview of the Family Smoking Prevention and Tobacco Control Act." Retrieved from http://www.fda.gov/TobaccoProducts/
63. *The Drinking Driver Problem: Where to From Here* (1981, January). A Report to the Board of Trustees of the Alcoholism Council of Cincinnati.
64. Devine, J. (2009, July 17). "A Brief History of DWI Law." Retrieved from http://ezinearticles.com/?A-Brief-History-of-DWI-Law&id=1335561.
65. Ibid.
66. BAC Calculator. Downloaded February 6, 2009. http://www.scienceservingsociety.com.
67. National Highway Traffic Safety Administration. (2009). *The Visual Detection of DWI Motorists.* Available from http://www.nhtsa.gov.
68. *The Drinking Driver Problem: Where to From Here* (1981, January).
69. Ibid.

70. Blocker J. (2006, February). "Did prohibition really work? Alcohol prohibition as a public health innovation." *American Journal of Public Health*, 96(2), 246.

71. Lender and Martin, (1987). *Drinking in America: A history*. New York, NY: Free Press.

72. Blocker J. (2006, February). "Did prohibition really work? Alcohol prohibition as a public health innovation." *American Journal of Public Health*, 96(2), 244.

Chapter 4

Policy Options

> *Government exists to protect us from each other. Where government has gone beyond its limits is in deciding to protect us from ourselves.*
>
> President Ronald Reagan

> *The right to swing my fist ends where the other man's nose begins.*
>
> Supreme Court Justice Oliver Wendell Holmes

The current debate on drug policy tends to revolve around the legalization issue. The proponents of legalization view drug problems as more the result of drug prohibition than the effects of the drugs themselves. In their view, legalization, moving drugs to a legal regulated market status, would have overall positive benefits.

Washington Post writer, Kathleen Parker, succinctly makes the legalization case in a column on the Michael Phelps marijuana photo controversy. In early 2009, Phelps, perhaps the greatest swimmer in Olympic history, was photographed at a South Carolina party holding a bong pipe. In writing about the controversy that erupted following publication of the picture, Parker noted:

Arguments against prohibition should be obvious. When you eliminate the victimless "crime" of drug use, you disempower the criminal element. Neutering drug gangs and cartels, not to mention the Taliban, would be no small byproduct of decriminalization. Not only would state regulation minimize toxic concoctions common on the black market, but also taxation would be a windfall in a hurting economy.[1]

There is no shortage of people who take strong exception to the legalization case. The Drug Enforcement Administration (DEA) argues that only a small minority of Americans use illegal drugs, that drug use itself is more the root cause of crime than drug marketing, and that America's drug problem would grow substantially worse under a framework of legalization.[2]

The drug policy debate is a mix of philosophy, strategy and pragmatism with economic factors thrown in as well. At its heart, the discussion is a debate on the role of government in people's lives. Those who view drug use, as Parker describes, a "victimless" activity, staunchly defend the individual's right to use drugs as a freedom of choice issue. Jeffrey Miron, describing the Libertarian position on drug legalization, states:

> The fundamental tenet of the libertarian perspective on drug legalization is that individuals, not governments, should decide who consumes drugs. This stems in part from the libertarian assumption that most individuals make reasonable choices about drug use. It also reflects the libertarian view that, even when individuals make bad decisions about drug use, government attempts to improve these decisions create more problems than they solve. Thus, libertarians accept that some drug use seems irrational and self-destructive, but they believe prohibition creates far more harm than drug use itself. Moreover, they do not think reducing drug use an appropriate goal for government policy except in situations where such use has direct and substantial costs to innocent third parties.[3]

Miron nicely captures the policy dilemma. Drug use *is* an individual choice; however, Miron's depiction of that drug use which is "irrational and self-destructive" is an articulate description of drug addiction, which clearly meets Miron's standard of "direct and substantial costs to innocent third parties." Miron would have policy-makers intervene in these limited circumstances. Advocates of a more activist government role perceive the damage caused by drug use as far more broad than their libertarian colleagues and thus believe that more significant governmental intervention is appropriate.

In broad terms, there are three approaches to drug control. At the one end is prohibition—criminalizing possession, use, manufacture, transportation and sale of the drug. This general description covers the current policy approach to the popular illegal drugs including marijuana, cocaine, heroin, and methamphetamine. The second approach is legalization—the drug is used within a legal framework that may include product quality standards and monitoring, tax policy, advertising restrictions, age restrictions, and a plethora of others. This regulatory mechanism as the agent of control describes the current approach to tobacco and alcohol. Although use is legal, criminal penalties may apply for certain drug related behavior—including driving under the influence, open flask, and sale to minors.

The third general approach is captured by the term decriminalization. In a pristine decriminalization approach, drug activity is neither illegal per se, nor is it controlled and monitored by regulatory bodies. In much of the literature and debate on "legalization," little distinction is made between decriminalization and legalization. Some advocates would involve the government in the production and sale of drugs in a minimalist fashion. As an example, the anti-prohibitionist group, Law Enforcement Against Prohibition (LEAP), advocates that the government should "import or produce the drugs and control them for quality, potency, and standardized measurement."[4]

In theory, under decriminalization, people would manufacture, distribute, buy/sell and use drugs free of criminal sanctions. As the drugs would not be legal, there would not be government controlled manufacture, distribution, etc. but the activity would take place in an uncontrolled black market situation which the government would largely ignore.

Within each of these general approaches, there is substantial variation. Criminalized drug activity covers trafficking (manufacture, distribution, sale), drug possession, and possession of drug instruments (needles, crack pipes). Sale of drugs is considered more heinous than simple possession or purchase and heavier criminal penalties may be applied based on the quantity of drugs seized. Repeat offenses bring increased penalties. Criminal penalties typically vary by drugs. In most locales, marijuana use or possession is treated as a misdemeanor, while possession of cocaine or heroin is a felony.

An increasingly popular tactic used against drug traffickers makes use of civil court actions. Seizing money, vehicles, houses, and other property from drug suspects has become a common tool in the struggle against dealers. The tactic, known as Asset Forfeiture, is believed to provide a further deterrent to drug dealing and has also become, in some cases, a substantial source of revenue for local police agencies.

Criminal penalties on the possession and sale of alcohol are still in place in the United States. Alcohol remains illegal in about 10% of the United States. Almost 50% of Mississippi counties are dry, 55 of the 120 Kentucky counties are dry, and 74 of the 254 counties in Texas are dry. The rules in these dry areas vary—some allow private clubs to sell alcohol, some prohibit alcohol possession, and some prohibit even transport of alcohol through the county.[5]

For legal drugs, the regulatory structure is complicated with sets of rules that vary from jurisdiction to jurisdiction. These rules cover everything from product composition, advertising, packaging and labeling, tax policies, hours of sale, and a host of others. A review of some of the Alcohol Beverage Control (ABC) measures in different states illustrates the voluminous nature of rules governing alcohol use across the country. For example, in Alabama, beer containers may not exceed 16 ounces, sale is prohibited in 26 of Alabama's 67 counties, but possession and consumption is allowed in those 26 counties. In

Arkansas, only wine produced within the state can be sold in supermarkets. In Oklahoma, beer over 3.2% alcohol and liquor/wine over 4% alcohol may only be sold at room temperature. In Utah restaurants, no alcohol is sold unless food is also purchased. In New York, liquor stores must be owned by individuals who are required to live within a certain distance of the store.[6]

Some states have more permissive policies. Louisiana has no open container law nor any prohibition against public intoxication. Likewise, public intoxication in Nevada is not only permitted but state law forbids local jurisdictions from passing any ordinances against it. Within New Jersey, Atlantic City is exempted from most state alcohol regulations and retailers there are allowed to sell alcohol 24 hours a day.[7]

As with tobacco, alcohol taxes are an important part of the regulatory control playbook. Research has conclusively demonstrated that increasing alcohol taxes reduces drinking among all alcohol consumers including heavy drinkers.[8] A study of alcohol tax increases in Alaska over a nearly 30-year period found tax rates related to not only consumption but also to drunk-driving arrests, drunk and disorderly arrests, and overall alcohol related death rates.[9]

A group of strategies that does not fit neatly within the prohibition—legalization continuum is harm reduction measures. Harm reduction advocates believe that "drug use is part of our world and chooses to work to minimize its harmful effects rather than simply ignore or condemn them."[10] Some common harm reduction strategies targeted at drug problems include provision of clean needles for IV drug users; providing safe injection locations for users; testing of drugs to ensure safety; and teaching addicts and those close to them how to provide emergency treatment for overdose victims.

All of these strategies come with some controversy. For two decades, national law has expressly forbidden the use of federal funding to support needle exchange. In July of 2009, the House of Representatives passed legislation removing that ban. However, to the chagrin of needle exchange advocates, the outright ban was replaced with language that prohibits needle exchange programs within 1000 feet of schools, daycare centers, swimming pools, and video arcades. As a practical matter, the 1000 foot restriction would make needle exchange programs in urban areas difficult if not impossible. William McCool, Political Director of the AIDS Action group noted, "In an urban environment, that really is a restriction on almost anywhere. It would preclude the use of needle exchange in the areas that need it most."[11]

The debate in the Congress captures the policy dilemma. Supporters of the exchange concept noted several studies including a World Health Organization report that concluded that "There is compelling evidence that increasing the availability and utilization of sterile injecting equipment by IDUs (injecting drug users) reduces HIV infection substantially."[12] Those against the needle exchange program included Representative Todd Tiahrt, a Republican from Kansas, who argued that drug users are "dependent on a lifestyle that only leads to destruction, and ... I personally don't want to be part of that destruction."[13]

This debate on harm reduction strategies is not limited to illegal drugs. The campaign against drunken driving has made extensive use of harm reduction tactics, most notably the designated driver program. The Designated Driver program was originally proposed by the Harvard University Alcohol Project in 1988 and has since gained widespread approval by the American public.[14] National beer companies, particularly Anheuser-Busch, have invested significant resources into support of designated driver programs. Major League Baseball, using the tie-in with their Designated Hitter Rule, has also been a supporter. Anheuser-Busch's latest effort includes a partnership with NASCAR featuring driver Richard Petty as the spokesperson. Anheuser-Busch has spent an estimated $750 million on designated driver programs since 1982.[15]

Designated driver programs are not without their critics. In a fashion analogous to the opposition directed at needle exchange programs, critics argue that designated driver programs encourage drunkenness by "winking at heavy drinking by anyone but the driver."[16] Just as needle exchange programs act to reduce the risks of IV drug use, designated driver programs lower the risks of alcohol abuse, and in the eyes of some, increase abuse potential.

There is a wide-ranging menu of policy options, including harm reduction tactics, which might be deployed to control drug problems. Selection of the right policy mix begins with an understanding of the dimensions of the problems presented by each drug. What might be an effective tactic for one drug could be ineffective for another drug.

From the larger strategic viewpoint, the public expects governmental policy to be effective, fair, and cost efficient. If drug policy initiatives fall short in any of these areas, citizens should not only expect change but should demand it.

EFFECTIVENESS

No one would argue for an ineffective policy so the debate often comes down to dueling statistics. Mark Twain famously stated there are three kinds of lies—lies, damn lies, and statistics. Proponents of a certain policy initiative are certain to interpret statistics to support their position. Opponents may use the exact same statistics in an attempt to discredit a proposal they do not like

It is also important to recognize there is a significant emotional component in much of the debate about drugs. For many people, drug use, in and of itself, is morally repugnant and they will react strongly against any proposal that does not strongly condemn all use of drugs. In the early 1980's, I was the Executive Director of a local chapter of the National Council on Alcoholism, an agency that, among other things, was involved in organizing drug/alcohol prevention programs in schools. One of our board members, a teacher at a local high school, was working with the school administration to implement a prevention program when some strong parent resistance to the proposal emerged. The debate was not on the effectiveness of the program, its cost nor any of a myriad of issues one might have expected to encounter. Under the goals section in the program literature was a claim that the program would reduce the percentage of students who would try marijuana. Opponents of the program latched onto this phrase, interpreting it to mean that the program would not demand 100% abstinence among the students and therefore the program was derided as "soft on drugs."

Measuring effectiveness begins with a decision about the nature of the problem we are facing. There are a few areas of agreement. Most everyone would agree that children using drugs should be prohibited. Zimring and Hawkins argue that a primary goal of drug policy should be protection of children and youth:

> If there is a universal proposition that is accepted by all parties to the debate on drugs, it is that children and youth should not have unregulated access to potentially harmful psychoactive substances Even the most ardent libertarians assent to this.[17]

But even this level of agreement begins to deteriorate as the discussion moves away from children and toward adolescents and young adults. Consider the current controversy over the 21 year old drinking age.

Advocates, most notably MADD, stress the lives saved by the move to a national 21 drinking age. In 1984, the federal government imposed the 21 drinking age across the country by threatening to withhold highway funds to those states that did not implement the 21 drinking age. Research on the issue appears

---

Drug Theft Leads to Beheading

Martin Alejandro Cota-Monroy's body was found Oct 10 in a Chandler (Arizona) apartment—his severed head a couple feet away. One man suspected in the killing has been arrested, and a manhunt is under way for three others. Detectives are focused on whether the men belong to a Mexican drug cartel, and they suspect that Cota-Monroy's killing was punishment for stealing drugs. The brutal nature of the killing could be designed to send a message to others within the cartel.[18]

---

persuasive. Studies dating back to the 1970's support the conclusion that a minimum legal drinking age of 21 (MLDA21) prevents alcohol-related deaths and injuries among youth and when the age was lowered, injury and death rates increase and conversely, when the age was raised, injuries and deaths decline.[19]

Not everyone agrees that the MLDA21 movement has been a success. A group of college presidents, led by John McCardell, President Emeritus of Middlebury College, argues strongly that the MLDA21 has had limited impact and have formed a non-profit organization, Choose Responsibility, to advocate for changes to the policy. McCardell and his colleagues argue that under the MLDA21 law, fewer young people may be drinking, but binge drinking has increased. They argue further that the MLDA21 is widely disregarded and breeds disrespect for the law.

Choose Responsibility also disputes the notion that the 21 drinking age has been an unqualified success. They note that traffic fatalities began to decline nationally in 1969 and the teen fatality rate decreased 19% between 1968 and

1975, long before the 21 drinking age too effect. They attribute the decrease in injuries and fatalities more to safety belts and air bags than to the drinking age change. They also note that the number of age-specific driving fatalities closely mirrors the proportion of those drivers in the population thus discounting the effect of the 21 drinking age.[20]

Researchers Miron and Tetelbaum provide a very insightful perspective on the minimum drinking age controversy. Some states went to a 21 minimum age prior to the federal mandate and others only changed when threatened with the loss of federal highway funds. Miron and Tetelbaum compared traffic fatality rates in those states that adopted the change on their own with those who were coerced by the Federal Government. The results of the analysis were surprising.

> Virtually all the life-saving impact of the MLDA21 comes from the few early-adopting states, not from the larger number that resulted from federal pressure. Further, any life-saving effect in those states that first raised the drinking age was only temporary, occurring largely in the first year or two after switching to the MLDA21.[21]

This sort of dichotomy characterizes almost all areas of the drug policy debate. To more effectively frame the debate, consensus on defining exactly what we are trying to accomplish will be helpful. An example from a drug-related problem solving effort by police illustrates the dilemma.

> I got a call from a citizen He told me, "On my way to work this morning, at 7:30 a.m., I got flagged down by some guys trying to sell drugs at McMicken and Vine Streets Here I was, in my business suit and Honda—it just seems like it's out of control." I think everybody would agree it was out of control. I called the lieutenant at our drug unit. "I just got a citizen complaint. This guy says dealers were trying sell him drugs at 7:30 this morning at Vine and McMicken."
>
> The lieutenant exploded. "Jesus Christ! In the last six months," (I heard the sounds of paper shuffling), "we made over 200 arrests at that corner." We both got quiet as the reality of the problem set in. Judging by the numbers, our efforts at that corner had been tremendous—lots of arrests, and, no doubt, a serious amount of drugs confiscated. But the problem persisted. It was apparent that our response, arresting a lot of people, wasn't working."[22]

It has been said that the definition of insanity is to continue the same behavior, expecting different results. Unfortunately, that is a description of much of our effort in the "War on Drugs." Nearly every day, the media will report on a record drug seizure or the arrest of the latest "drug kingpin." Rarely noted is the fact that these drug seizures cause barely a ripple in the street availability of drugs or that the next "kingpin" in-waiting takes over the organization and business continues as usual. This phenomena is particularly vivid at the retail (street) level.

In every major city, the police will, on a daily basis, make multiple arrests of individuals for drugs. Sometimes, large operations, or "sweeps" that target a particular drug location will be organized. The drug business at that location will be disrupted for a few hours or a few days before a new set of dealers, or the old ones out on bail, resume their operations. Describing these operations as a success is misleading, and most police officials have long recognized we cannot arrest our way out of the drug problem. Posing with large amounts of drugs, cash, and weapons may be a public relations success, but the impact on the problem is usually minimal at best.

How then should we measure success? Using the example above, "Success is when the citizen drives by and there are no dealers trying to sell him drugs."[23] Filling the jails with people for drug offenses is not an indicator of success but instead is a sign of our failure to effectively deal with the problem .

FAIRNESS

Fairness, somewhat like beauty, is in the eye of the beholder. Reasonable people will disagree on the fairness of many aspects of drug policy. Unfortunately, the history of American drug policy is clearly tainted by racism, vestiges of which continue to color the discussion.

What is believed to be the first American anti-drug law was imposed in San Francisco in 1875. That law targeted the smoking of opium and opium dens which were mostly utilized by Chinese laborers. The law was clearly directed at Chinese immigrants and driven by the fear that white women were being lured to their moral ruin in the opium dens.[24]

At the turn of the century, cocaine was targeted partly on the belief that black men using the drug might engage in violent sexual rampages against white women. Newspapers in the 1900's warned of "Negro Cocaine Fiends" with superhuman strength.[25]

Laws on marijuana stem from similar origins. In Congressional hearings in 1937, Harry Anslinger, head of the federal Bureau of Narcotics, testified in support of marijuana restrictions due to the drug's violent effect on "degenerate races."[26]

While the overt racism described is part of a sad history in American race relations, the impact of today's drug laws continues to fall heaviest on racial minorities. The history of prison sentencing related to crack cocaine is a good illustration.

In 1986, in the midst of media-fueled political hysteria about crack cocaine, Congress passed the Anti-Drug Abuse Act. The law mandated harsh penalties for low-level drug offenses and established different penalties for powder cocaine versus crack cocaine. For sale of crack amounting to about two sugar packets, a five year mandatory sentence was imposed. To reach the five year sentence threshold for sale of powder cocaine, a sale of 100 times that quantity was required.[27] The stated intent of the law was to "impose tough sentences on high-level drug market operators, such as manufacturers or heads of organizations distributing large quantities of narcotics, and serious traffickers with a substantial drug-trade business."[28] The reality was that the penalties "apply most often to offenders who perform low-level trafficking functions, wield little decision-making authority, and have limited responsibility."[29] These penalties fell heaviest on African American offenders. Despite government data that show drug use rates roughly equivalent among ethnic groups, 81% of federal crack cocaine defendants in 2006 were African American.[30]

The pattern is not just one that is found in federal sentencing The figures are daunting:

> *Whites constitute 72% of all drug users in the US.*
> *Blacks constitute 13.5% of all drug users in the US.*
> *But. . . 37% of those arrested for drug violations are Black*
> *African-Americans comprise almost 60% of those in state prisons for drug felonies.*[31]

The impact on the black community is difficult to overstate. Consider that the incarceration rate for black males in South Africa under the apartheid regime in 1993 was 851 per 100,000. Yet in 2008, the United States incarceration rate for black males was 6,667 per 100,000.[32]

Fortunately, the latest figures show a slowing of this trend. The 2009 report by the Sentencing Project found the number of African-American inmates in state prison for drug crimes had declined by over 20% between 1995 and 2005. While this was greeted as positive, the same study found the overall number of drug offenders imprisoned increased from 251,200 in 1999 to 253,300 in 2005.[33]

Crafting drug policy positions that will be largely supported by the diverse groups in our society will take patience and wisdom. Rightly so, fairness will be a major focus of the discussion. On this basis, it is difficult to support some of the current policies and in fact, it stretches credulity to view the incarceration statistics and still maintain that race is a non-factor.

COST EFFICIENT

In the middle of the worst recession in the last half-century, the financial implications of drug policy alternatives are taking on added importance. New York State has had some the most punitive drug laws in the country and economic considerations are driving some proposed changes. In 2009, Governor Dave Patterson stated, "Since 1973, New York has had the harshest drug laws in the country, and they have simply not worked."[34] Patterson noted that the state's prison population had soared from 20,000 in 1973 to 60,000 currently and that most inmates are non-violent drug offenders who could be treated much more cheaply than the cost of incarceration. Poughkeepsie City attorney William Tendy is among supporters of the proposed changes. "Our prisons were exploding with people with drug problems, and they were costing the state a fortune," Tendy said "If it can be shown someone is not selling drugs but has a drug problem, they should get treatment instead of jail. It's amazing it took this long but thank God it happened."[35]

The current recession has also sparked efforts to legalize marijuana as a tax revenue measure. California Assemblyman Tom Ammiano has introduced legislation that would legalize marijuana and bring in an estimated billion dollars annually in state tax revenue from sale of the drug.[36]

The actions described above in New York and California highlight two of the major economic considerations in drug policy considerations. Criminalizing behavior and then processing offenders through the criminal justice system is expensive. The exact costs of the current effort to control illegal drugs are difficult to quantify but there is no doubt it is substantial. Some critics contend that legalizing drugs would save taxpayers $70 billion per year.[37]

Criminal Justice costs include not only law enforcement costs, but expenses related both to prosecution and defense as many defendants are indigent. Court costs are also significant as defendants are processed through the system. As the sanctions become more punitive, they become more costly. Community control measures like probation and home incarceration are less expensive than local and state prisons.

Cost estimates that simply measure the costs of processing and institutionalizing offenders provide only a portion of the financial picture. Much of the true cost of criminalizing behavior is hidden. A criminal record becomes a significant barrier to future employment and economic success. When incarceration occurs, taxpayer support of the offender's family as well will often follow.

There are also cost considerations on the demand side of the drug policy equation. Prevention programs are more cost effective than treatment programs. Outpatient programs are less costly than inpatient programs and proper matching of the individual with the program will enhance cost effectiveness.

Drug prohibition opponents focus heavily on the tax revenue potential inherent in drug legalization. It is certain that significant revenue could be generated through drug tax policy. What is less certain is the financial costs associated with any legalization protocol. Tax revenue from both tobacco and alcohol are substantial but neither covers the cost of the problems related to tobacco or alcohol consumption. Focusing solely on the potential revenue of legalization addresses only half the equation.

Discussion

It is difficult to review the historical record on drug prohibition effort and label it effective. The bottom line results include thousands of people incarcerated, large and increasing governmental expenditures but with use patterns, drug price, purity measures and addiction rates largely unaffected.

Between 1970 and 2005, drug arrests in the United States quadrupled. Total drug arrests in 1970 amounted to less than half a million people. By 2005, that number had jumped to nearly two million. Arrests for marijuana were nearly half of the total drug arrests and of the marijuana related arrests, 88% were for simple possession.[38]

The costs of prosecuting drug wars has also grown exponentially with an estimated one trillion dollars spent since 1970.[39] The latest installment is a 2009 promise of a $700 million U.S. aid package to Mexico to fight traffickers on the border.[40]

Price and purity measures are one metric used by the government to evaluate success in drug interdiction efforts. In theory, drugs are like many other commodities. If supply is diminished, the price will increase and the quality or purity will decrease. The DEA tracks price and purity measures as an indicator of their success in keeping drugs from American streets. LEAP founder Jack Cole, a retired New Jersey State Officer who spent most of his career as an undercover drug officer, notes that he was buying $3 bags of heroin in 1970 that were 1.5% pure. By 1999, this cost had dropped to an inflation adjusted 80 cents/bag and the purity of the heroin had jumped to 38%.[41]

Cole's reporting on the price/purity of heroin is consistent with government data related to cocaine. The DEA began collecting price and purity information in 1981 and reported the value of a gram of pure cocaine at $600. In 2006, the price for that same gram of pure cocaine had dropped to $135, a level that has varied little since the early 1990's.[42]

Data reported by the United Nations seems to confirm the pattern of increasing purity and lower prices. A 1999 report found purity and price measures with discouraging results both in Europe and the United States. "Over the past decade, inflation-adjusted prices in Western Europe fell by 45% for cocaine and 60% for heroin. Comparative falls in the United States were about 50% for cocaine and 70% for heroin."[43]

Drug use trends will vary over time; however, the long term results are discouraging. Peak years for teen marijuana use in the United States were 1979 and 1980 when over 60% of high school seniors reported use of marijuana. This level of use gradually declined to a low of 32% in 1992, but use began to increase again, reaching 49% into the new century before declining once again in 2007.[44]

Use patterns for other illegal drugs fluctuate as well. In the 2007 University of Michigan survey of high school students, 1.5% reported at least one use of heroin. This compares to 41.8% of the students for marijuana, 3.4% for LSD, 7.8% for cocaine and 3% for methamphetamine.[45] These figures appear to vary over the years related as much to the faddish nature of drug use as to policy changes. The use of methamphetamine is an example. This is a drug that was not even tracked in the Michigan survey until 1990 when 2.7% of seniors reported use of "crystal meth" or "ice." By 1999, almost 8% of seniors were reporting use of methamphetamine.[46]

Drug addiction rates appear unchanged over the past quarter century. In 1979, an estimated 1.3% of the population was believed to be addicted to drugs.[47] Using current population figures and government reports on addiction, Robinson and Scherlen estimated that the same level of addiction, 1.3% of the population, existed in 2002.[48]

None of these figures address alcohol or tobacco. However, consumption of both alcohol and tobacco have declined over the same time period (1979-2002). In 1979, the American per-capita consumption of alcohol was estimated at 2.75 gallons, based on those 15 years of age and older. In 2002, per-capita consumption had dropped to 2.2 gallons yearly. While the 2002 consumption level was down significantly from 1979, it has increased since reaching a low of 2.14 in 1998.[49]

As noted earlier, decreasing tobacco consumption is one of the public health success stories of the last fifty years. The smoking rate has been cut in half since 1965 and the adolescent rate of use has declined significantly as well.

While progress has been evident on tobacco and alcohol related problems, it should be evident that simply legalizing a substance is not the same as solving problems related to that drug. The percentage of Americans classified as alcohol dependent is estimated at nearly 5%, a number which has grown over the past ten years.[50] While progress has also been made on the tobacco front, the health care costs associated with tobacco addiction continue to escalate and a significant percentage of Americans continue to use tobacco

Changing the legal status of a drug may change the particular mix of social problems that a specific drug's use generates. Some of the trade-offs may in fact be socially desirable but any policy changes should be implemented with a clear understanding that today's solutions may well create tomorrow's problems. Evaluating these changes with a critical eye on potential effectiveness, fairness and cost benefits will work to ensure positive and sustainable results.

NOTES

1. Parker, Kathleen(2009) *Sometimes a Smoke is Just a Smoke* Postwriters.com, February 13, 2009.

2. DEA, (2003) *Speaking Out Against Drug Legalization*, U.S. Department of Justice, Drug Enforcement Administration, May, 2003.

3. Miron, Jeffrey.(2004) "Liberal versus Libertarian Views on Drug Legalization," Published in *The New Prohibition: Voices of Dissent Challenge the Drug War*, Sheriff Bill Masters, ed., Accurate Press, 2004.

4. Cole, Jack (2009) *This is Not a War on Drugs—it's a War on People*, http://leap.cc/cms/index.php?name=Content&pid=29. Downloaded 3/13/2009.

5. Hanson, David (2009) *Dry Counties* Alcohol Problems and Solutions, http://www2.potsdam.edu/hansondj/controversies/1140551076.html. Downloaded 3/11/2009

6. Wikipedia (2009) "Alcohol Laws of the United States." http://en.wikipedia.org/wiki/Alcohol_laws_of_the_United_States_by_state. Downloaded 3/13/2009.

7. Ibid.

8. Wagenaar, Alexander, Salois, Matthew & Komro, Kelli(2009) *Effects of Beverage Alcohol Price and Tax Level son Drinking: A Meta-Analysis of 1003 Estimates from 112 Studies* Addiction, Volume 104, Issue 2January 15, 2009: 179-190.

9. Wagenaar, Alexander, Maldonado-Molina, Mildred, Wagenaar, Bradley (2007) "Effects of Alcohol Tax Increases on Alcohol-Related Disease Mortality in Alaska: Mime-Series Analyses from 1976 to 2004." American Journal of Public Health, Http://www.ajph.org/cgi/content/abstract/AJPH.2007.131326v1?maxtoshow=&HI Accessed 3/13/09.

10. Harm Reduction Coalition (2009) *Principles of Harm Reduction* http://www.harmreduction.org/Downloaded August 25, 2009.

11. Lillis, Mike (2009) "Congress Looks to Lift Two-Decade Ban on Federal Needle Exchange Funds." *The Washington Independent (online)*, July 9, 2009.

12. WHO (2004) *Effectiveness of Sterile Needle and Syringe Programming in Reducing HIV/AIDS among Injecting Drug Users* World Health Organization, Switzerland, 28.

13. Lillis, 2009.

14. Johnson, Elaine (1995) "Cheers for the Designated Driver Program," *Safety and Health*, The National Safety Council, Itaska, IL, 1995.

15. McWilliams, Jeremiah (2009) "Budweiser Launches New Responsibility Campaign." St. Louis Dispatch, May 26 2009.

16. CSPI (1996), *Paying the Piper: The Effect of Industry Funding on Alcohol Prevention Priorities* Center for Science in the Public Interest, Washington, D.C. http://www.cspinet.org/booze/ppstudy.htmlDownloaded August 25, 2009.

17. Zimring, F& Hawkins, G(1992)*The Search for Rational Drug Control*. New York, NY: Cambridge University Press, 115.

18. Sakal, Mike (2011, March 5) "Chandler police link beheading to theft of marijuana from Mexican cartel." East Valley Tribune.com Retrieved from http://www.eastvalleytribune.com/local/cop_shop/article_4dba9618-4540-11e0-98da-001cc4c03286.html.

19. Wagenaar AC (1993) "Minimum Drinking Age and Alcohol Availability to Youth: Issues and Research Needs." Hilton ME, Bloss G, eds. *Economics and the Prevention of Alcohol-Related Problems.* National Institute on Alcohol Abuse and Alcoholism (NIAAA) Research Monograph No25, NIH PubNo93-3513Bethesda, MD: NIAAA; 1993:175-200.

20. Choose Responsibility (2000) "Arguments Against Legal Age 21," http://www.chooseresponsibility.org/against_legal_ageDownloaded 4/1/09.

21. Miron, Jeffery and Tetelbaum, Elina (2009) "The Dangers of the Drinking Age." http://www.forbes.com/2009/04/15/lowering-legal-drinking-age-opinions-contributors-regulation.htmlRetrieved November 4, 2009.

22. Rahtz, Howard (2001)*Community-Oriented Policing Handbook* . Monsey, NY Criminal Justice Press: 80-81.

23. Ibid, 81.

24. Schaffer, Clifford (2009) *Basic Facts about the War on Drugs*
Downloaded April 2, 2009 United States Sentencing Commission(2002) *Report to Congress: Cocaine and Federal Sentencing Policy*, May 2002. http://www.druglibrary.org/schaffer/library/basicfax.htm, 45.

25. Ibid.

26. Ibid.

27. The Sentencing Project (2009)"Federal Crack Cocaine Sentencing." Retrieved from Http://sentencingproject.org/doc/publications/dp_CrackBriefingSheet.pdf.
28. Ibid, 2.
29. Ibid.
30. Ibid.
31. LEAP (2010.) "End Prohibition Now Slide Show." Retrieved from http://www.google.com/search?q=Whites+constitute+72%25+of+all+drug+users+in+the&ie=utf-8&oe=utf-8&aq=t&rls=org.mozilla:en-US:official&client=firefox-a.
32. Ibid.
33. Moore, Solomon(2009) "Fewer Blacks in Prison for Drugs." N.Y. Times, April 14, 2009.
34. Spector, Joseph (2009)"New York passes drug law reform." Retrieved from http://www.poughkeepsiejournal.com/section/news.
35. Ibid.
36. Eskenazi, Joe (2010) "Legalize It: Ammiano to Introduce Legislation Monday to Allow Pot – and Tax It." San Francisco Weekly http://blogs.sfweekly.com/thesnitch/2009/02/legalize_it_ammiano_to_introdu.php downloaded April 11.
37. LEAP, 2009.
38. Ibid.
39. Ibid.
40. Strobel, WP(2009, March 27) "Clinton says US shares responsibility for Mexico's drug violence." The Christian Science Monitor Retrieved from http:www.csmonitor.com/2009/0327/p99s01-woam.html.
41. LEAP, 2009.
42. Goodman, Joshua(2007) "U.S. Cocaine Prices Drop, Purity Increases." Associated Press, April 27, 2007.
43. United Nations Office for Drug Control (1999)*Global Illicit Drug Trends.* United Nations Publication (ISBN 92-1-148122-8, p86.
44. Johnston, LD., O'Malley, PM., Bachman, JG., & Schulenberg, JE(2011)*Monitoring the Future national survey results on drug use, 1975-2010Volume I: Secondary school students* Ann Arbor: Institute for Social Research, The University of Michigan, 734 pp.
45. Ibid.
46. Ibid.
47. Kane, John. (2004) "Policy is Not a Synonym for Justice." In *The New Prohibition: Voices of Dissent Challenge the Drug War,* Edited by Sheriff Bill Masters, St. Louis: Accurate Press, 2004, Chapter 5, p45.
48. Robinson, Matthew Band, Renee and GScherlen (2007) *Lies, Damned Lies, and Drug War Statistics: A Critical Analysis of Claims Made by the Office of National Drug Control Policy*, State University of New York Press, New York, 2007.
49. NIAAA (National Institute on Alcohol Abuse and Alcoholism), (2009) "Apparent Per Capita Ethanol Consumption for the United States, 1850–2006(Gallons of Ethanol, Based on Population age 15 and Older.)" http://alcoholism.about.com.
50. Ibid

Chapter 5

An International Perspective

> *It has become increasingly hard to justify the highly punitive nature of current U.S. policies, which contrast so sharply with other Western nations.*
>
> Dr. Peter Rueter, Rand Corporation.
> In Congressional Testimony, May 19, 2009

Many countries around the world struggle with drug problems. Over 100 countries have official national drug policies and they vary greatly. The policies often differ as a result of authorities trying to respond to the specific problems associated with a particular drug. Almost all countries will vary policy based on a particular drug, with marijuana policy often widely different from policy on cocaine or heroin. All countries make a distinction between users of a drug and drug traffickers. Throughout the world, traffickers are subject to more significant penalties, including capital punishment, than users will face. India, China, Pakistan, Iran and Thailand are among those countries where drug traffickers may face the death penalty.[1]

Policy on drug possession also varies across the world. The general trend is more lenient treatment for possession offenses. Even those countries with traditionally more repressive policies have moved away from criminal penalties and toward drug treatment as an option for addicted users. Iran, as an example, has recently recognized addiction as a health problem and is experimenting with methadone maintenance for heroin addicts. In 2004, Russia decriminalized drug possession for personal use. Individuals caught with small quantities of drugs now face administrative sanctions (fines, etc.) rather than criminal penalties. Users may also be sentenced to community service.[2]

A significant change in direction came from Mexico in August of 2009, a change that came with surprisingly little opposition or even comment from Washington, D.C. In 2009, Mexico's government acted to decriminalize possession of small quantities of not only marijuana, but all illegal drugs. Rather than arrest people caught with drugs, police officials now "will give them the address of the nearest rehab clinic and advise them to get clean."[3]

Drug legalization advocates view the Mexican action and Washington's muted reaction as evidence of coming change in American drug policy. Mexican legislators had passed a nearly identical bill in 2006; however, after American protests, the bill was quashed. The Obama administration's reaction has been non-committal, with Drug Czar Kerlikowske taking a "wait and see" stance.[4] Mexican officials believe the new policy is overdue. "There is a growing opinion that the use of force has simply failed to destroy the drug trade and other measures are needed," says Mexican political analyst José Antonio Crespo.[5]

Drug policy alternatives in European countries have generated most of the policy discussion in America. Europe has generally more liberal policies than the United States, but even within the European Union there are a tremendous variety of options in play. Drug policy in Europe ranges from the Netherlands and Portugal, some of the most liberal in the world, to Sweden, with a drug policy framework more conservative than the United States. Portugal in particular is a country that has in the past few years reworked its national drug policy with some interesting and relevant results.

Despite the diversity of policy options, there is broad agreement on some issues. A review of drug policies finds wide diversity among the countries of the European Union and yet growing agreement in some policy areas.[6] There are a few clear trends in European Union drug policy. The most notable is an increasingly clear demarcation between drug users, viewed as people suffering from an addiction and in need of treatment, and drug traffickers, viewed as criminals.[7]

Possession of drugs for personal use has been decriminalized in many parts of Europe. In countries where criminal penalties are still imposed, the penalty structure has grown less severe. Reclassifying drug possession for personal use as an administrative violation rather than criminal violation has been implemented by a number of countries, including Russia, Portugal, Switzerland and Luxembourg. In 2001, Luxembourg made marijuana "possession (along with transportation and acquisition for person use)" administrative offenses.[8] In Switzerland, possession of any drug for personal use is subject only to administrative sanctions and in Russia, as of 2004, possession of up to ten doses of any drug for personal use is subject only to administrative fines.[9]

Even where criminal penalties for possession offenses have been retained, they are rarely used. In Germany, prosecutorial policy is that possession of small amounts of any drug is not prosecuted. In Denmark, police issue a "caution" or warning to those caught with cannabis while those caught with heroin will receive a warning and the drug will be confiscated. In France, prosecutors ignore cases of simple possession under a stated policy that includes a provision that prison for drug offenses should be used "only as a last resort."[10] Possession of small amounts of any drug are not prosecuted in Holland, and cannabis is openly consumed in a network of licensed Coffee Houses.

Many countries are making increased use of harm reduction strategies. The growth of substitution treatment, using government produced heroin or methadone, along with needle exchange programs, has been credited with the reduction of overdose deaths and infectious diseases. These harm reduction measures are widely available and the "general European trend is one of growth and consolidation of harm-reduction measures."[11] France, Spain and Portugal have all documented reduced drug-related deaths and levels of infectious disease attributed to harm reduction measures.[12]

Another trend is the creation of alternatives to punishment for addicts identified in the court system. Drug courts have been implemented in Ireland, the United Kingdom, and Norway, and are being considered in Malta. In Portugal, drug offenders are referred to a committee composed of a lawyer, doctor, and social worker in what are called "commissions for the dissuasion of drug use."[13] A partial list of countries where offenders are offered treatment as an alternative to punishment includes Spain, Hungary, Latvia Bulgaria, Romania, Finland, the Netherlands, Greece and Turkey. While the details of the programs vary, the trend of diverting drug users away from the criminal justice system is widespread.[14]

Recognizing a distinction between users and dealers and diverting users from the criminal justice system are two rather clear trends that are somewhat counterbalanced by a focus on protecting the public from drug users. Penalties for drug-taking behavior that endangers the public have been strengthened in much of Europe. A prime example is policy as it regards driving under the influence of drugs. Belgium, Spain, France, Portugal and Latvia are among countries that have recently increased criminal penalties for driving under the influence.[15] Increased drug testing in the workplace and new governmental powers to control drug related public nuisances (bars, drug houses) are further examples of the movement to protect the public from drug problems.

While there are potential lessons in the review of policy struggles in many European countries, a review of three in particular, the Netherlands, Sweden, and Portugal, seem particularly relevant. The Netherlands has a long history of liberal drug policies and is often cited by advocates on both sides of the legalization issue. Sweden is on the opposite end of the spectrum with a drug policy framework more conservative than that of the United States but with reportedly better results. Portugal is noteworthy as it has recently shifted its drug policy emphasis with some results that demand attention.

THE NETHERLANDS

Drug policy in the Netherlands has drawn both praise (for example, "Dutch Drug Policy: A Model for America"[16]) and scorn (in works such as "Holland's Half-Baked Drug Experiment").[17] In designing its policy response to drug problems, the Netherlands has taken a radically different path than both the United States and most of its fellow European countries.

Prior to the 1960's, Netherlands drug policy was not wildly different from other countries. Student riots in 1966 and accusations of excessive force by the Amsterdam police in quelling the riots led to a re-examination of police priorities.[18] In the firestorm of criticism directed at police following the student riots, police deemphasized drug enforcement in general and chose not to enforce marijuana laws in some areas of Dutch cities frequented by young people. Marijuana was not legalized but the authorities adopted a policy of refraining from prosecution "to avoid a situation in which consumers of cannabis suffer more damage from criminal proceedings than from use of the drug itself."[19]

The idea of protecting cannabis consumers is also at the heart of the network of the infamous Coffee Houses in the Netherlands. The Coffee Houses are primarily found in Amsterdam, which accounts for about 50% of the estimated 700 Coffee Houses nationally. Of the approximately 350 Coffee Houses in Amsterdam, about 100 are clustered in the city center, a location with a brisk tourist trade in both drugs and prostitution. One important principle underlying the Coffee Houses is separation of the markets. The belief is that by providing marijuana in a controlled setting like the Coffee Houses, users will be less likely to come into contact with the illegal drug market and access to heroin, cocaine and other more dangerous drugs.

Under the Dutch system, marijuana remains an illegal drug. Possession and use of marijuana is a misdemeanor but possession for personal use, defined as five grams or less, is not prosecuted. Sale of the drug outside the Coffee Houses is not allowed. Coffee Houses are allowed to stock a maximum of 500 grams of marijuana.[20] Import, export and production of large amounts of marijuana is considered a serious offense subject to prosecution.[21]

The Dutch drug policy and its offspring, Coffee Houses, are not without their critics. Larry Collins, co-author of *Freedom at Midnite, Is Paris Burning?* and other historical works, has been one of the bluntest and most eloquent critics of the Dutch drug policy. Collins views the results of Dutch drug policy as a failure and a warning for other nations considering Dutch type drug policy.[22]

In a 1999 article in *Foreign Affairs* magazine, Collins describes Holland as the "drugs capital of western Europe."[23] Collins quotes police officials throughout Europe who view Holland's drug policy as a major factor in their own country's drug problem:

> 'Holland has become the place for drug traffickers to work,' states a senior officer at Her Majesty's Customs and Excise. 'It's central. You've got guys there who have access to any kind of drug you want,

smugglers who can deliver it for you to Liverpool or London. And it's an environment which is relatively trouble-free from a criminal's point of view. It's ideal, and it has become a magnet for our criminal types.' As a senior French narcotics officer puts it, 'Holland is Europe's drug supermarket. Drugs of all kinds are freely available there. The price is cheap. Your chances of getting caught with them are minimal, and you can carry them home across our customs-free borders without a care.'[24]

Collins attributes much of the problem to what he describes as the "coffee-shop mentality" that characterizes Holland's drug policy approach. Collins quotes a French police official who says, "If you want to do drugs, Holland is the place to do them. The light sentences they hand out [and] the liberal attitude of their judges have resulted in an explosion in the number of international trafficking groups operating out of Holland."[25]

Another problem highlighted by Collins is the movement to a higher potency marijuana named "Nederwiet." With no government controls on cannabis potency, Dutch growers have been free to develop marijuana plants with ever stronger THC concentrations. The Nederwiet cannabis accounts for an estimated 70% of the marijuana consumed in Dutch coffee shops and has a THC content of 35%, ten times higher than the marijuana cultivated in the 1970's. Collins reports that Nederwiet "has a smooth taste, and many aficionados judge it the best marijuana on the market."[26]

Despite the criticisms of Collins and others, there is no lack of support either within Holland or outside the country for the Dutch policy approach. In a response to the Collins article in *Foreign Affairs*, supporters of the Dutch approach dispute Collins' claim of the potency of Dutch cannabis quoting an independent Dutch Drug Monitoring Center study that found, "most Dutch users actually prefer the milder strains of marijuana and that those who do smoke the stronger stuff use less of it."[27] Supporters of the Dutch policy also note lower rates of marijuana use and lower rates of drug addiction in Holland than in the United States.[28]

While harm reductions strategies have had only a minor role in United States drug policy, they are a central element in the Dutch approach. Duncan and Nicholson note the Dutch policy is based on three principles. The first is separation of the markets, with access to marijuana in Coffee Houses serving as the main tactic. The second is the provision of low threshold treatment programs, and the third is normalization of treatment.[29]

The low threshold treatment principle means removing as many barriers to treatment as possible to encourage addicts to enter treatment. Minimal paperwork and minimal demands on the addict are characteristic of this approach. For heroin addicts entering methadone treatment, the only requirement is that the methadone be taken on site. The hope is that over time, the addict will choose a more demanding program, engage in group or individual therapy, and work toward long term recovery. An example of the Dutch treatment approach is the Methadone by Bus project. The bus, a mobile methadone clinic, makes the rounds of Amsterdam daily. Addicts are given their methadone along with clean syringes and condoms.[30]

The third thrust of the Dutch treatment approach is the normalization of treatment principle. The aim of the policy is the "reintegration of addiction treatment into routine medical practice."[31] To accomplish this movement of addiction treatment into routine medical practice, the Dutch government created a network of 200 general practice physicians who prescribe methadone to a limited number of addicts as part of their practice. About 40% of all the Methadone patients in Holland are now treated by private physicians, each treating on average, no more than four or five addict patients. The policy allows "addicts to obtain their medicine without advertising the fact that they are addicts and discourages the development of a 'junkie' peer group, with drug culture norms, at the treatment site."[32]

SWEDEN

At roughly the same period of time that the Netherlands was moving toward a liberalization of its drug policies, Swedish drug policy moved in the opposite direction. Swedish policy developed largely under the influence of Nils Bejerot, a physician sometimes referred to "as the founding father of Swedish drug control policy."[33] Swedish policy continues to be driven by Bejerot's focus on criminalization of drug users and development of a strong cultural bias against drug use. Today, the Swedish model is "driven by a policy of zero-tolerance and is guided by a vision of a drug-free society. The strategy focuses on targeting the user—a supply and demand philosophy that suggests that customers at the bottom of the pyramid form the base for the dealers at the top. Remove that bottom layer—and the pyramid comes crashing down."[34]

Since the incorporation of Bejerot's vision into Swedish drug policy in the late 1960's, government reliance on criminal action against drug users has only strengthened. In the 1970s, Sweden had adopted a policy, widespread in Europe, of not charging individual drug abusers caught with small amounts of illegal drugs. This changed in 1980 when "new directives to prosecutors ruled out any waiver of charges unless the amount possessed for personal use was so small that it could not be subdivided. ...Moreover, charges for possession of heroin, morphine, opium or cocaine, should, in principle, never be waived at all."[35]

In 1988, Sweden increased its penalties for drug offenses with both minimum and maximum sentences increased. In 1982, drug policy was again modified, this time allowing the state to coerce drug abusers into treatment.[36] The policy, as it was modified in 1988, allows the state to commit a person to treatment for up to six months. For the commitment to take place, the legal standard is that the drug abuser is "running an obvious risk of destroying his life" and "it can be feared that he will inflict serious damage on himself or on someone with whom he has a close relationship."[37]

In 1993, Sweden took a step beyond criminalizing drug possession and made drug abuse itself a criminal offense. Thus, the law allows a Swedish police officer, who has reasonable grounds to suspect drug use, to take an individual into custody, even in the absence of any drug possession, and "to undertake a bodily examination in the form of urine or blood specimen test."[38] Critics of Swedish policy are particularly critical of this expanded police authority:

> In Stockholm, police will chase drug users all through the night and collect them in their vans from the streets, and from the cafés. Trained special police can go into a bar, merely look one in the eye and arrest him or her, then drag them into police headquarters where blood is extracted from them against their will. Police violence on the drug using population is carefully nurtured in Sweden as a necessary element in the witch hunt against this alien evil, drugs.[39]

Supporters of the expanded police power describe it as a way to "provide opportunities to intervene at an early stage so as to vigorously prevent young persons from becoming fixed in drug misuse and improve the treatment of those misusers who were serving a sentence."[40]

The Swedish approach to drug treatment is also radically different from that of the Netherlands. While Dutch policy has focused on reducing the stigma associated with drug addiction and minimizing barriers to treatment, Sweden has taken a more punitive approach. Swedish policy, as articulated by Nils Bejerot in the 1960's, continues to emphasize coercive treatment. Bejerots himself was dismissive of the value of voluntary treatment. "Voluntary treatment is about as intelligent as voluntary prison," Bejerots stated. "You just don't quit unless you are forced to do so."[41]

Yet some critics believe that the drug-related death rate is high in Sweden and that the punitive nature of Swedish drug policy is to blame. Dr. Ted Goldberg, of Stockholm University, commenting on the death rate of addicts in Sweden, notes:

> And of course it's not recreational consumers who are dying. Contemporary drug policy is in fact an important reason why so many problematic consumers die. Drug policy accomplishes this by driving users further out of society, by coercing them into meaningless and repressive treatment, by making them afraid to contact the authorities when, for instance, someone has overdosed...Drug policy, as it is today, is actually killing people—not saving lives.[42]

Sonja Wallbom, President of the Swedish National Association for Aid to Drug Abusers, and a supporter of increased harm reduction measures, agrees. "Punishment for drug addiction is very harsh—it's the wrong way to go. The message you send to addicts by criminalizing drug use is one that frightens them away from seeking treatment or from calling for an ambulance when an overdose occurs. People's lives are at stake."[43]

Supporters of the Swedish policy claim some successes. The United Nations 2007 report on Swedish drug policy notes "Drug use levels among students are lower than in the early 1970s. Life-time prevalence and regular drug use among students and among the general population are considerably lower than in the rest of Europe. In addition, bucking the general trend in Europe, drug abuse has actually declined in Sweden over the last five years."[44]

PORTUGAL

In the late 1990s, the country's growing drug problem became the focus of the Portuguese government. At that time, Portugal had a high level of drug-related problems, specifically increasing rates of HIV/AIDS and hepatitis, primarily due to a high level of heroin use. In 1999, Portugal had the highest rate of HIV amongst injecting drug users in the European Union. Use of marijuana was not a significant concern, as use rates were well below other European countries.[45]

In 1998, a National Commission was charged with the task of developing a national strategy to more effectively deal with the country's drug problem. The Commission's work led to a comprehensive plan, the National Strategy for the Fight Against Drugs, which was released in 1999. The National Strategy called for focusing police resources on traffickers while moving to a public health approach for drug users. This strategy was implemented in a 2001 overhaul of Portuguese law which decriminalized drug possession and dramatically altered the country's approach to drug problems. Most European countries have moved away from criminal prosecution of simple drug possession. However, these policies are not decriminalization, but more accurately, depenalization. Drug possession remains a criminal offense, but the policy is not to prosecute those found with small quantities of drugs. Portugal eventually completely decriminalized drug possession, making it an administrative offense, not a criminal offense. The exact wording of the law is, "The consumption, acquisition and possession for one's own consumption of plants, substances or preparations listed in the tables referred to in the preceding article constitute an administrative offence." The "tables referred to" in the passage above are a listing of psychotropic drugs and the phrase "for one's own consumption" is later defined as "being up to a 10 day supply."[46]

Drug possession is not legal but it is now handled through an administrative process with an emphasis on health care for addicts rather than a criminal justice process. Under the new law, those in possession of small amounts of illegal drugs, within the defined "10 day supply," are referred to local Commissions for the Dissuasion of Drug Addiction, or CDTs, as they are referred to in Portuguese. The CDTs represent an administrative process which cannot impose any criminal penalties.[47]

The CDTs consist of a three person panel—an attorney, a medical representative, and a drug treatment expert. Each CDT is supported by a staff of technical experts. Referrals to CDTs are most often initiated by police officers observing a drug violation. Instead of an arrest, the individual is cited to appear before the local CDT within 72 hours. Under the law, CDTs are to "gather in information needed in order to reach a judgment as to whether he or she is an addict or not, what substances were consumed, the circumstances in which he was consuming drugs when summoned, the place of consumption and his economic situation."[48] If the CDT determines the individual is not addicted, they can impose administrative sanctions including fines and community service. If the CDT determines the individual is an addict, that person is referred to drug treatment under the supervision of CDT staff but may also face a variety of other sanctions including "suspension of the right to practice a licensed profession (doctor, lawyer, taxi driver); a ban on visiting high-risk locales (nightclubs); a ban on associating with specified individuals; requiring periodic reports to the commission to show there is no ongoing addiction or abuse; prohibitions on travel abroad; and termination of public benefits for subsidies or allowances."[49]

The primary goal of the new policy, and the CDTs specifically, is to reduce stigma associated with criminal proceedings and encourage drug addicts to go into treatment:

> Each step of the process is structured so as to de-emphasize or even eliminate any notion of 'guilt' from drug usage and instead to emphasize the health and treatment aspects of the process.... Commission members deliberately avoid all trappings of judges, and the hearing is intentionally structured so as to avoid the appearance of a court.[50]

Police officers remain the key cog in the system and police conduct under the new law is the source of debate among Portuguese drug policy experts. Observers note:

> There are, to be sure, some police officers who largely refrain from issuing citations to drug users on the grounds of perceived futility, as they often observe the cited user on the street once again using drugs, leading such officers to conclude that the issuance of citations, without arrests or the threat of criminal prosecution, is worthless. Other police officers, however, are *more* inclined to act when they see drug usage now than they were before decriminalization, as they believe that the treatment options offered to such users are far more effective than turning users into criminals (who, even under the criminalization scheme, were typically back on the street the next day, but without real treatment options).[51]

Regardless of the level of police support for the CDT system, referrals by the police have increased steadily since 2001 leading one to believe that officers are increasingly supportive of the reform.[52]

While decriminalization was the centerpiece of the Portuguese policy, there were also other important elements. Anticipating a major influx of addicts into treatment, the capacity of treatment programs was greatly expanded. A new emphasis on drug education and prevention in schools was initiated, harm reduction efforts were increased and the police moved the focus of their enforcement efforts to large-scale trafficking organizations.[53]

Given the near hysteria that characterized some media reports on the new drug policy, it is appropriate to point out what did not happen in Portugal as a result of a change in the law. Early media reports mocked Lisbon as Europe's "most shameful neighbourhood" and its "worst drugs ghetto."

> This 'ultraliberal legislation,' said the foreign media, had set alarm bells ringing across Europe. The Portuguese were said to be fearful that holiday resorts would become dumping-grounds for drug tourists. Some conservative politicians denounced the decriminalization as 'pure lunacy.' Planeloads of foreign students would head for the Algarve to smoke marijuana, predicted Paulo Portas, leader of the People's Party. Portugal, he said, was offering 'sun, beaches and any drug you like.'[54]

The much ballyhooed drug tourism never materialized. "Roughly 95 percent of those cited for drug offenses every year since decriminalization have been Portuguese. Close to zero have been citizens of other EU states."[55]

Portugal's policy change appears to have been a success. The country's heroin problem, described as the worst in Europe in the late 1990s and which provided much of the impetus for the policy change, has dramatically improved. Since the inception of the new policy in 2001, newly reported cases of HIV/AIDS among drug addicts have declined dramatically. Newly diagnosed HIV/AIDS cases related to drug addiction have also fallen.[56]

Drug related deaths, the majority of which were heroin related, have also dropped. These figures are particularly impressive when compared to the pre-decriminalization statistics. Between 1989 and 1999, drug related deaths in Portugal increased ten-fold.[57] Yet between 1999 and 2003, drug related deaths in Portugal fell 59%.[58] Researchers believe the decline is attributable to the substantial increase in the number of heroin addicts entering treatment in the decriminalization period. The number of addicts in substitution treatment jumped from 6040 in 1999 to 14,877 in 2003.[59] These numbers have continued to increase and over 24,000 addicts were in substitution treatment as of 2008.[60]

The change in police focus to drug traffickers also appears to have been successful. The statistics are persuasive:

> Since the introduction of the new strategy, there have been considerable increases in the amount of drugs seized. There were increases of more than 100% in the amount of heroin, cocaine, cannabis and ecstasy seized between the four years 1995-1999 and the 2000-2004 period, even though the number of seizures decreased. This could indicate that the Portuguese authorities have successfully refocused their supply reduction efforts on large-scale operations.[61]

The post decriminalization picture on drug use in Portugal is less clear. Surveys of high school students aged 16-18 found a pattern of increasing marijuana use comparing 1999 to 2003. At the same time, heroin use among this age group decreased.[62] Referrals to the CDTs also reflect an increase in the percentage of cannabis referrals accompanied by a drop in heroin referrals.[63]

Later studies, reviewing the changes five years after decriminalization, provide a much more positive picture. Surveys of 7th, 8th, and 9th graders compared lifetime use rates in 2001, the year decriminalization was implemented, and 2006. In every drug category, use declined. Cannabis use rates dropped by about a third and cocaine, amphetamines and ecstasy use all declined by approximately fifty percent.[64] Surveys of 10th, 11th, and 12th grade students found similar outcomes.[65]

Portuguese authorities point to drops in the usage rates among the 15-19 year old population, which appear particularly significant. This is the age group in which drug initiation typically occurs and the rate among this age group has declined since decriminalization in 2001.[66]

It is also instructive to view the drug use statistics for Portugal in the context of other countries within the European Union. Reported drug offenses in the EU for all drugs, with the exception of heroin, increased in the period from 2001 to 2005 with reported cocaine offenses increasing by over fifty percent.[67] Since Portugal had decriminalized possession offenses, there is not a direct comparison available. However, this is the same period in which reported drug use in Portugal, including cocaine use, was declining. For marijuana, the most popular drug in all European Union

---

Child Drug Soldiers

They have barely reached puberty, but already Rio's teenagers have picked up weapons to fight in the ongoing drug wars. Brazilian gangs prefer using children to do their dirty work—their prison sentences are shorter. Ricardo M. was 11 years old when he killed a person for the first time. It was night, and about 20 boys had gathered at the highest point in the favela. With hunting rifles and assault weapons slung over their shoulders and handguns stuck into the waistbands of their Bermuda shorts, it looked as if a war were about to break out in this poverty-stricken neighborhood on the outskirts of Rio de Janeiro. After an evening spent snorting cocaine, the boys were high and completely uninhibited. A whimpering teenager, his face disfigured from the beating he had just taken, knelt at their feet. He had been tortured with cigarettes and blades. For the boys, he was nothing but what they called an "X9"—a traitor who had informed on a gang member. The penalty was death. The gang leader pressed a .38 caliber revolver into Ricardo's hand. Holding the heavy weapon with both hands, Ricardo held it against the offender's head and pulled the trigger. The other boys applauded and slapped Ricardo on the back. He had passed the initiation rite for membership in "Terceiro Comando," Rio's second-largest criminal organization. From then on he would be a "soldier" of the Mafia. Together with the other boys, Ricardo dragged the dead boy into a ditch, poured gasoline on the body and lit a match. "I felt nothing," he says today. "I was too high."[68]

countries, for the period 2001-2005, Portugal had the lowest lifetime prevalence rate in the EU.[69]

DISCUSSION

Attributing changes in drug use solely to governmental policy changes is risky at best. Drug use patterns and problems may change even in the absence of any policy initiative. Hughes and Stevens note that "it is notoriously difficult to measure drug use and related problems accurately... The causal link between drugs, death, disease and crime is not direct."[70]

Comparing drug problems cross-culturally also brings an added level of complexity. Diverse data collection methods, multiple standards for defining drug problems and accessing the variety of bureaucratic structures holding the data all make these studies a difficult proposition. At the same time, dismissing potential strategies from other countries simply on the grounds they may not work in the United States closes the door to a wealth of tested tactics that may in fact have significant potential in the United States.

There is growing consensus in some policy areas. Drug addicts are increasingly being diverted from the criminal justice system. The experience in Portugal and the Netherlands demonstrates that policies bringing addicts into treatment combined with expanded harm reduction measures can have a measureable impact on drug related deaths and the rate of HIV/AIDS infections. Swedish policy, from a different perspective, also recognizes the role that addicts play in the context of broader drug problems. Heavy use of criminal sanctions is the primary tactic to dissuade addiction in Sweden, but even Swedish governmental studies question the effectiveness of this tactic. In a 2000 evaluation study of the effectiveness of Swedish criminal justice system measures, the National Council for Crime Prevention of Sweden concluded that "based on available information on trends in drug misuse there are no clear indications that criminalization and an increased severity of punishment has had a deterrent effect on the drug habits of young people or that new recruitment to drug misuse has been halted."[71] While Swedish authorities continue to use criminal prosecution and coercive treatment as a primary tactic, nonetheless, the goal of increasing the number of addicts into treatment remains the same.

In 2009, Mexico decriminalized drug possession, a decision that was at least in part driven by the corruption of police officers "who frequently shook down people by threatening them with arrest."[72] Under the new Mexican law, users who are caught by the police are to be referred to treatment programs. Those caught for the third time will be forced to attend treatment.[73]

While a number of states have replaced criminal sanctions with administrative penalties for drug offenses, Portuguese authorities took a further step. For personal possession of drugs, the new policy replaced the criminal justice process with an administrative/health focused process, the CDTs. The CDT process in Portugal is much more aggressive than the policy of simply ignoring personal possession offenses. This active approach accounts, at least in part, for the huge increase in the number of addicts in Portuguese treatment programs.

It is important to note that neither Portugal nor the Netherlands have legalized drugs. Marijuana users in the Netherlands may purchase and use cannabis in Coffee Houses, but outside the Coffee House system, marijuana is still illegal. As marijuana remains an illegal product, there are neither controls on the potency of the drug nor controls on other ingredients added by trafficking entrepreneurs. This lack of control contributes to the mishmash of cannabis products; drinks, food products and smokeable marijuana like the Nederwiet strain, both celebrated and criticized for its high potency level. None of the consumer protection that would be in place with a legal product is available. Further, while both Portugal and the Netherlands have adopted a form of de facto legalization, neither has taken advantage of the revenue possibilities that would come with full legalization.

With full recognition of the problems inherent in cross-cultural comparisons, there are aspects of the European experience that might be considered by U. S. policymakers. Failure to acknowledge that other countries are having more success in controlling their drug problems represents a denial of the facts similar to the denial characteristic of drug addicts. A 2009 review comparing drug problems in different countries serves as a reminder of the ineffectiveness of current U.S. policy.[74]

For cocaine use, the United States had the highest rate of lifetime use among young adults, a rate three times higher than the Netherlands and more than five times higher than Portugal. For marijuana, the United States rate of use was exceeded only by Canada and represented a use rate nearly triple that of Portugal.[75]

On problem drug use, the Netherlands had the lowest rate of problem drug users and the United States had the highest rate, over five times the Dutch rate. Similarly, the United States had the highest rate of drug related deaths, again nearly five times the Dutch rate.[76]

Using the criminal justice system as the primary response to drug problems has resulted in the United States incarcerating more of its citizens than any other country in the world. In 2006, nearly two million Americans were jailed for drug offenses, with 82.5% of these prisoners incarcerated for possession offenses.[77]

The United States spends more money on controlling drug problems than any other country with law enforcement costs representing 64.5% of the total funds expended.[78]

There are several lessons to be gleaned from a review of the drug policy of other countries:

- Increasing the number of addicts in treatment has a positive effect on the level of drug problems. Whether this is done via low threshold treatment entry standards, active outreach, or a new administrative structure like CDTs in Portugal, the result will be fewer drug-related problems.

An International Perspective 65

- Stigma appears to be a major barrier for people needing drug treatment, In Portugal, moving from a criminal justice model to an administrative/health care model drastically increased treatment demand. The increasing use of drug courts in the United States is a half-step in this direction. Treatment capacity will need to be greatly expanded to handle the higher number of patients.

- Harm reduction tactics can reduce HIV/AIDS rates among IV drug users. These tactics will be controversial and will likely only be successful where the local population supports them.

- Where decriminalization occurs, enforcement efforts against traffickers may be more successful as those resources formerly devoted to possession offenders are redirected.

- The separation of markets principle underlying marijuana use in the Dutch Coffee House network is effective in limiting access to other illegal drugs and might be considered as part of a policy framework in the United States.

- A policy of not prosecuting possession only offenders or total decriminalization may have some positive results but it fails to utilize the regulatory control benefits inherent in legalization. It leads to the uncontrolled distribution of dubious and possibly dangerous drug products like Niederweit in Holland. The current situation in California around medical marijuana products is a clear example of what occurs in an unregulated situation.[79]

- A policy short of legalization may indeed have benefits, however, it will miss the economic benefits that accompany a legal product. Tax revenue is only part of the economic potential in a legalization framework.

Discussing any changes in U.S. drug policy, including legalization, will fly in the face of forty years of the conventional thinking that any such discussion is to be "soft on drugs" as though that is some sort of character defect. It is noteworthy that the Portuguese authorities, in making the dramatic shift in that country's drug policy, did not view it as surrender to drug problems:

Portuguese decriminalization was never seen as a concession to the inevitability of drug abuse. To the contrary, it was, and is, seen as the most effective government policy for reducing addiction and its accompanying harms. That criminalization was *exacerbating* the problem, and that only decriminalization could enable an effective government response.[80]

It is not being "soft on drugs" to point out that the current approach is ineffective and wasteful. In the conclusion to the CATO Institute Report on the change in Portugal's drug policy, Glen Greenwald notes, "Around the world, it is apparent that stringent criminalization policies do not produce lower drug usage rates. If anything, the opposite trend can be observed. The sky-high and increasing drug usage rates in the highly criminalized United States, juxtaposed with the relatively low and manageable rates in decriminalized Portugal, make a very strong case for that proposition."[81]

The time is overdue for national discussion of our country's drug problems and policy alternatives. In entering this discussion, the policy experience of other countries should be included within the conversation. While the experiences, both positive and negative, may not easily generalize to the situation in the United States, quick dismissal of these options would be both arrogant and intellectually dishonest.

NOTES

1. DrugPolicy Around the World (2009). Http://www.drugpolicy.org/global/. Retrieved 7/29/2009.
2. Ibid.
3. Grillo, Joan. (2009) "Mexico's New Drug Law May Set an Example." *TIME.com*, August 26, 2009. http://TIME.com. Downloaded 8/26/2009.
4. Ibid.
5. Ibid.
6. EMCDDA (2006). *Annual Report 2006: The State of the Drugs Problem in Europe*. Office for Official Publications of the European Communities, Luxembourg.
7. Ibid.
8. Transform, (2006). "After the War on Drugs: Options for Control." *Transform Drug Policy Foundation*. www.tdpf.org.uk. Downloaded October 8, 2009, 41.
9. Ibid, 41.
10. Ibid, 41.
11. EMCDDA, *Annual Report 2006*, 32.
12. Ibid, 32.
13. Ibid, 23.
14. Ibid.
15. Ibid.
16. Duncan, D.F., & Nicholson, T. (1997). "Dutch Drug Policy: A Model for America?" *Journal of Health and Social Policy, 8*(3), 1-15.
17. Collins, Larry. (1999). "Holland's Half-Baked Drug Experiment." *Foreign Affairs*, Vol. 78, No. 3. May/June, 1999. New York, N.Y. http://www.foreignaffairs.org/. Downloaded September 13, 2009.
18. Punch, M. (1985) *Conduct Unbecoming: The Social Construction of Police Deviance and Control*. London: Tavistock, 1985.
19. Engelsman, E. L. (1989) "Dutch Policy on the Management of Drug-Related Problems." *British Journal of Addiction*. 1989; 84: 211-218.
20. IDPC (2009). "The Netherlands Reviews its Tolerant Approach to Drug Policy." *International Drug Policy Consortium*, http://www.idpc.net/alerts/review-dutch-drugs-policy-summary. Downloaded September 13, 2009.

21. Ibid.
22. Collins, 1999.
23. Ibid.
24. Ibid.
25. Ibid.
26. Ibid.
27. Cohen, Peter, and Reinarman, Craig. "Human Nature – A Response to Larry Collins." *Foreign Affairs Magazine* Website. http://www.foreignaffairs.org/. Retrieved September 13, 2009.
28. Ibid.
29. Duncan and Nicholson, 2009.
30. Ibid.
31. Ibid.
32. Ibid.
33. United Nations Office on Drugs and Crime (2007). *Sweden's Successful Drug Policy: A Review of the Evidence.* United Nations, New York, NY, 12.
34. Porter, Anders. (2008). "Sweden's Tough Stance on Drugs up for Debate." March 23, 2008. Downloaded from http://www.sweden.se/eng/Home/Work-live/Government-politics/Reading/Not-so-user-friendly-debating-Swedish-drug-policy/wede.
35. UNODC, *Sweden's Successful Drug Policy,* 14.
36. Ibid.
37. Ibid, 15.
38. Ibid.
39. Cohen, Peter. (2006). "Looking at the UN, Smelling a Rat." *CEDRO*, www.cedro-uva.org/. Downloaded September 30, 2009: 6-7.
40. UNODC, *Sweden's Successful Drug Policy,* 16.
41. Porter, "Sweden's Tough Stance."
42. Cohen, "Looking at the UN," 6.
43. Porter, "Sweden's Tough Stance."
44. UNODC, *Sweden's Successful Drug Policy,* 5.
45. Hughes, Caitlan and Stevens, Alex. (2007). "The Effects of Decriminalization of Drugs in Portugal." *The Beckley Foundation,* www.internationaldrugpolicy.net. Downloaded September 15, 2009.
46. Greenwald, Glenn. (2009). *Drug Decriminalization in Portugal: Lessons for Creating Fair and Successful Drug Policies.* CATO Institute. Washington, D.C., 3.
47. Hughes and Stevens, (2007). "The Effects of Decriminalization."
48. Greenwald, (2009). *Drug Decriminalization*: 5-6.
49. Ibid: 3-4.
50. Ibid, 4.
51. Ibid.
52. Ibid.
53. Hughes and Stevens, (2007). "The Effects of Decriminalization."
54. *Economist*, (2009). "Portugal's Drug Policy: Treating, not Punishing." Lisbon, August 27, 2009.
55. Greenwald, (2009) *Drug Decriminalization,* 6.
56. IDT (2006). Institute on Drugs and Drug Addiction of Portugal. "The National Situation Relating to Drugs and Dependency," 2005 Annual Report (2006).
57. Greenwald, (2009) *Drug Decriminalization,* 6.
58. IDT, (2006). "The National Situation."

59. Tavares, LV, Graça, PM, Martins, O & Asensio, M (2005). *External and Independent Evaluation of the "National Strategy for the Fight Against Drugs" and of the "National Action Plan for the Fight Against Drugs and Drug Addiction – Horizon 2004."* Portuguese National Institute of Public Administration, Lisbon.
60. *Economist*, (2009) "Portugal's Drug Policy."
61. Hughes and Stevens, (2007). "The Effects of Decriminalization."
62. Tavares et al., (2005). *External and Independent Evaluation.*
63. IDT, (2006)"The National Situation."
64. Greenwald, (2009). *Drug Decriminalization*, 12.
65. Ibid.
66. Ibid, 14.
67. EMCDDA, (2007). *Annual Report 2006*, 25.
68. Glusing, Jens (2007, February 28. "Violence in Rio de Janeiro: Child Soldiers in the Drug War." Retrieved from http://www.essex.ac.uk/armedcon/story_id/000448.htmlsjpigal online, 3/2/2007
69. Greenwald, (2009). *Drug Decriminalization*, 21.
70. Hughes and Stevens, (2007). "The Effects of Decriminalization."
71. National Council for Crime Prevention (2000). "The Criminalization of Narcotic Drug Misuse -- An Evaluation of Criminal Justice System Measures" (English summary), Stockholm, 42.
72. Lacey, Marc (2009). "In Mexico, Ambivalence on a Drug Law." *The New York Times*, New York, NY. August 23, 2009.
73. Ibid.
74. Degenhardt, Louisa; Christopher Hallam; and Dave Bewley-Taylor. (2009) *Comparing The Drug Situation Across Countries: Problems, Pitfalls And Possibilities.* The Beckley Foundation, Sydney, Australia, September, 2009.
75. Ibid.
76. Ibid.
77. Ibid.
78. Ibid.
79. Welch, William. (2009). "Booming Medical Pot Sales Concern Officials." *USA Today*, September 30, 2009, On-Line Edition. http://www.usatoday.com/news/nation/2009-09-29-medical-marijuana_N.htm. Downloaded October 14, 2009.
80. Greenwald, (2009). *Drug Decriminalization*, 10.
81. Ibid, 27.

Chapter 6

Drug Abuse—The Damage Done

> "A single death is a tragedy; a million deaths is a statistic."
>
> Joseph Stalin

> "Much confusion results from treating all illegal drugs as a single policy target."
>
> Dr. Peter Rueter
> Congressional Testimony
> May 19, 2009

A parent discovers his teenager's stash of marijuana; a supervisor struggles to help an alcoholic employee; a family gathers around the deathbed of their father, a victim of lung cancer—America's drug problem is a messy compendium of different substances, each bringing a somewhat unique set of outcomes. The consequences of drug use include early death, health problems, criminal behavior, family issues, and more.

While illegal drugs tend to monopolize policy discussions, the control of alcohol and tobacco problems represents a serious challenge. Alcohol and tobacco policy also provides lessons on the potential of a governmental regulatory system to control drug problems within a legalized framework. To begin to get a handle on the dimensions of America's drug problem, a look at the most abused drugs (legal and illegal) and their related issues is a good starting point.

LEGAL DRUGS—ALCOHOL

Beer at the ballpark, happy hour, tailgating at a football game, a few drinks before dinner, a fraternity party—drinking alcohol is as American as apple pie. From humorous beer commercials to the neighborhood bar, alcohol is an accepted part of our cultural life. Yet alcohol problems, with the exception of the periodic high profile drunk driving incident, generally stay under the radar of American social consciousness.

Alcohol remains one of the country's deadliest drugs. Alcohol related deaths in the U.S. exceed 100,000 each year, including deaths from health problems (notably cirrhosis of the liver, heart disease, and cancer), drunk driving deaths, alcohol overdoses and accidental falls and deaths. Alcohol problems are a major contributor to escalating health care costs with problem drinkers spending four times more days in the hospital than non-drinkers.[1]

An estimated 14 million Americans are afflicted with a drinking problem. More teens—fifty percent of high school seniors by one survey—use alcohol more than any other drug. Binge drinking remains a major concern, with 32% of high school seniors reporting drunkenness within the past thirty days.[2]

The number one drug associated with criminal violence is alcohol with an estimated forty percent of violent victimizations involving alcohol. Further, forty percent of convicted offenders in all crime categories reported being drunk or drinking at the time of their offense.[3]

Alcohol plays a major role in family violence episodes. National statistics identify alcohol in two-thirds of domestic violence incidents,[4] but in my experience as a police officer, even this estimate seems low. Through my years as a street officer and responding to scores of incidents of domestic violence, I can recall only a handful in which the offender and/or the victim were *not* drinking.

Costs of alcohol abuse to the American economy were estimated at $184.6 billion dollars in 1998, including medical related costs, costs associated with alcohol related crime, and costs due to traffic crashes and fires.[5]

LEGAL DRUGS—TOBACCO

About 70.3 million Americans describe themselves as current tobacco users. The majority of them are cigarette smokers, followed by cigar smokers, pipe smokers, and lastly, smokeless tobacco users. Tobacco is second only to alcohol in total number of users.[6]

The health problems related to tobacco use are enormous. Nearly half a million deaths each year result from tobacco use, with one out of every six U.S. deaths directly related to tobacco. About 8% of the deaths are victims of second hand smoke.[7] Tobacco related deaths exceed the number of deaths attributed to alcohol, cocaine, heroin, homicide, suicide, car accidents, fire, and AIDS *combined*. Over 90% of all lung cancer cases are caused by tobacco use.[8] Economically, the health care costs attributed to tobacco related problems is a staggering $75 billion.[9]

Nicotine, the active ingredient in tobacco products, is one of the most addictive substances known to man. Nicotine acts in the human brain in a fashion similar to other drugs of abuse and over half of the current smokers try to quit each year with only 6% of them succeeding.[10]

Tobacco use does not have the intoxication effect found in other drugs of abuse. Users report pleasure associated with tobacco, but the immediate physical and psychological effects associated with many other drugs are not present. For example, tobacco use does not cause psychomotor impairment that endangers people in driving situations. Tobacco use has not been associated with violence in the same manner as other drugs, even though individuals attempting to stop their tobacco habit will describe, sometimes at great length, the emotional and physical discomfort they are experiencing.

Fortunately, tobacco use is declining. Although the number of users remains high, there has been a fifty percent decrease in the incidence of smoking since 1965. Cigarette smoking among adolescents shows a similar decline. In the late 1970's, about three-quarters of high school seniors reported they had smoked cigarettes. This number has gradually declined with forty-six percent of 2007 seniors reporting smoking, a decrease of forty percent.[11]

ILLEGAL DRUGS—MARIJUANA

Marijuana remains the country's most heavily used illegal drug. According to an annual survey done by the University of Michigan, nearly fifty percent of American children have tried marijuana by the time they reach the 12th grade.[12] This survey, done every year since 1975, is considered one of the most accurate indicators of national drug use.

The survey has documented marijuana use among teens that is consistent over the years. Peak years for teen marijuana use were 1979 and 1980 when over 60% of high school seniors reported use of marijuana. This level of use gradually declined to a low of 32% in 1992, but use began to increase again, reaching 49% into the new century and declining once again to 42% in 2007.[13]

The potency of marijuana has increased over the years. Researchers have documented an increased concentration of Tetrahydrocannabinol or THC, the psychoactive ingredient in marijuana. Estimates on marijuana potency vary, with some sources reporting dramatically increased potency over that of the 1970's version of the drug. Some reports estimate that today's marijuana registers five times the strength of the 1970s drug, while other reports estimate the strength to be as high as twenty-five times that of earlier decades.[14]

Using marijuana brings a variety of health problems. As marijuana is smoked, many of the health problems common to smoking cigarettes are also prevalent. Also, the practice of holding the smoke in the lungs to enhance the high, increases the exposure to the toxic compounds found in marijuana. Studies of confiscated marijuana find it contains more than 400 different chemical compounds, the long term effects of which are unknown.[15]

Marijuana users face increased risks of developing cancer of the head and neck as well as cancer of the lungs and respiratory tract. Marijuana smoke contains significantly heavier concentrations of carcinogenic hydrocarbons than does tobacco smoke.[16] Marijuana was also the third most commonly cited drug in hospital emergency room admissions, behind alcohol and cocaine.[17]

Marijuana is also implicated in traffic deaths. Reports on fatal accident victims found six to eleven percent testing positive for THC. Research by the National Highway Traffic Safety Administration found moderate doses of marijuana impairing driving skills, and using alcohol in conjunction with marijuana led to a level of impairment greater than the single drug use of alcohol or marijuana.[18]

ILLEGAL DRUGS—HEROIN

Of the illegal drugs commonly tracked, heroin is one of the drugs least used. In the 2007 University of Michigan survey of high school students, 1.5% of students reported at least one use of heroin. This compares to 41.8% of the students for marijuana, 3.4% for LSD, 7.8% for cocaine and 3% for methamphetamine.[19]

The National Survey on Drug Use and Health reports that an estimated 3.7 million people have used heroin some time in their life with 119,000 of them describing themselves as current users (within the previous month). The same survey estimates that 57% of the users could be classified as dependent.[20]

While the overall number of heroin users is relatively small, the consequences of their use are significant. For example, in 2006, police and health officials were confronted with an epidemic of heroin overdoses. The deaths were traced to heroin laced with Fentanyl, an extremely powerful opioid with a reported potency 50 times that of morphine.[21] Wayne County (Detroit) averaged four overdose deaths a day in May of 2006. Similar overdose deaths were also reported in Illinois, Wisconsin, New York, Pennsylvania, New Jersey, and Ohio. Fentanyl is a legal drug, prescribed for pain relief, and authorities were unable to determine whether the fentanyl in these cases was a legal product that had been diverted or fentanyl that had been produced in illegal clandestine labs.[22]

While the Fentanyl situation was an unusual occurrence, overdose death associated with heroin use constitutes a significant risk. Users never know the purity or additives in the substance they are injecting. As injection is the most common method of heroin use, health problems including HIV/AIDS, hepatitis, and infections are often present.[23]

The criminal violence associated with heroin is not the result of heroin intoxication. Heroin use is generally followed by a period of drowsiness with a slowed heart rate and respiration. Criminal activity comes as the user seeks the money to keep up the habit, which may cost as much as hundreds of dollars each day. The potential for addiction related to heroin use is high. A 2003 study classified 57% of current (past year) heroin users as "dependent."[24] Sudden withdrawal from heroin by heavy users may be medically dangerous, particularly among addicts in poor overall health.[25]

ILLEGAL DRUGS—COCAINE

Cocaine is derived from coca leaves and coca leaves have been ingested by human beings for thousands of years. The powder form of cocaine, cocaine hydrochloride, is chemically extracted from the coca leaves and has been used as a drug for over 100 years.

The two forms of cocaine in widespread use are powder cocaine and crack cocaine. Crack is the freebase form of the drug that is chemically derived from powder cocaine. Crack cocaine is processed from powder cocaine by mixing it with ammonia or baking soda and then heating it, which removes the hydrochloride, leaving a more pure form of cocaine. This form of cocaine may be smoked, giving the user a more immediate high, usually in less than 10 seconds. The name Crack is believed to originate in the crackling sound the drug makes as it is heated and smoked.[26]

It is estimated that over 40 million Americans have used cocaine, with over two million describing themselves as current users. The number of crack users in the U.S. is estimated at over 500,000.[27] The percentage of high school seniors reporting use of cocaine peaked at nearly 10% in 1998; but it has since declined to 7.8% of seniors reporting cocaine use in 2007.[28]

Cocaine use brings with it a variety of health problems that can vary depending on the method used. Smoking crack results in cardiovascular and respiratory problems including sudden death from heart attacks. Like with heroin, the body develops a tolerance to the drug requiring the user to use more of the drug to achieve a high. Users injecting the drug run risks of exposure to HIV/AIDS due to the practice of sharing "works" or needles. Users snorting the drug will develop chronic nosebleeds, and suffer a variety of nose and throat problems.[29]

Crack is considered more addictive than powder cocaine. This is due primarily to the different methods of use. Taking the drug by smoking it, as is done with crack, leads to the almost instant impact of the drug's euphoric effect, making it more highly reinforcing. Powder cocaine cannot be smoked and is generally "snorted" (taken in through the nostrils) or injected.[30]

There is also a marked difference in the duration of the high between crack and powder cocaine. The high from smoking crack lasts only 10-15 minutes, sometimes leading to a quick cycle of drug use and re-use. The high from injection or inhaling of powder cocaine typically takes longer to occur and lasts longer than the crack high.[31]

The behavior of the user while high is markedly different from heroin. While heroin use leads to a stupor like experience, most cocaine users experience the opposite effect. Users may feel energetic and mentally alert and some users report the drug helps them complete both physical and intellectual tasks more quickly. Users may also experience a decrease in appetite or the need to sleep.[32]

A relatively recent phenomenon has been the purposeful mixing of cocaine and alcohol. NIDA researchers have discovered that the biological processing of the two drugs through the liver manufactures a third substance, cocaethylene, which increases both the euphoric effect of the drugs and the user's risk of sudden death.[33]

ILLEGAL DRUGS—METHAMPHETAMINE

Methamphetamine is a relatively new arrival on the national scene but one that has quickly emerged as a significant problem. In the annual survey of high school students, methamphetamine is not mentioned until 1990 when 2.7% of seniors reported use of "crystal meth" or "ice," both references to its appearance. By 1999, almost 8% of seniors reported use of methamphetamine in addition to the 4.8% who reported using crystal meth. In 2007, 3% of seniors reported using meth and 3.4% reported use of crystal meth.[34]

Like cocaine, methamphetamine is used in different forms. The smokeable form of methamphetamine is commonly referred to as "crystal" or "ice." The attraction of the smokeable form of meth is the almost immediate rush experienced. This high, unlike the very short-term high associated with smoking crack, can last up to eight hours.

Methamphetamine abuse has been geographically uneven with Hawaii, West Coast states, and more recently, some Mid-Western states, reporting meth related problems. Approximately 10 million Americans have used methamphetamine and 500,000 describe themselves as current users.[35]

The growing nature of the methamphetamine problem is illustrated by the number of people seeking emergency room assistance for methamphetamine problems as well as the number of people seeking drug treatment for a methamphetamine problem. The Drug Abuse Warning Network (DAWN) collects information on drug-related episodes from hospital emergency departments (EDs) throughout the nation. Per DAWN statistics, there was an increase of over 50% in the number of emergency room visits related to methamphetamine between 1995 and 2002.[36]

The number of people seeking treatment for methamphetamine problems has also increased dramatically. In 1992, about one percent of the total drug treatment admissions in the U.S. related to methamphetamine. By 2004, that figure had increased to 8%.[37]

Methamphetamine use brings with it significant health risks. The production process for methamphetamine is extremely dangerous. Users who try to "cook" their own methamphetamine risk death from explosions and/or suffocation from toxic fumes. In recent years, the production of methamphetamine has moved from individual users cooking their own product to large "super-labs" in Mexico.[38]

The addiction potential stemming from use of methamphetamine is high. Both the immediate euphoric effect and the longer term high experienced increase the addiction potential. Injection users who share needles risk exposure to HIV/AIDS. Those who smoke the drug may suffer a variety of respiratory problems. Psychological problems including hallucinations and psychotic episodes have been widely reported.[39]

In many parts of the country, meth has replaced cocaine as the focus of drug enforcement. In 2006, the White House Deputy Drug Czar, Scott Burns, called meth "the most destructive, dangerous, terrible drug that's come along in a long time."[41] A survey, reported by the Drug Prevention Network of the Americas, found 87% of US County Sheriffs seeing an increase in meth-related crime. A majority of the sheriffs identified meth as the main drug problem in their jurisdiction.[42]

> **Fight over drugs leads to murder**
>
> Loniesh Veasey, a Tacoma, Washington woman, was accused of killing her friend Ginny Thomas in what police described as an argument over drugs. Per Court documents, Veasey was high on crack and Thomas was using heroin when the argument erupted. The documents say Thomas stuck Veasey in the palm with a syringe and Veasey fought back with a razor blade wrapped in a tissue.[40]

A HYBRID PROBLEM—PHARMACEUTICAL DRUG DIVERSION

In the universe of drug problems, pharmaceutical diversion occupies a unique niche. A wide variety of drugs, easy access to those drugs, and a belief that because the drugs are legally manufactured they are less harmful, all factor into making prescription drug diversion a significant part of the national drug problem.

An estimated 2.5 million doses of prescription drugs are funneled into the illegal market each year.[43] Diverted drugs reach the user through a mind-boggling assortment of illegal channels. Straight-forward criminal action, the theft of drugs from manufacturers, wholesalers, pharmacies, and health care facilities accounts for some of the diverted drugs. While burglaries and robberies account for some of the drugs lost, close to 50% are diverted as a result of "insider" theft. As an example, in a 2002 case in Somerville, Massachusetts, a pharmacy intern was convicted of stealing more than 40,000 pills, including 16,000 Vicodin and nearly 6,000 Xanax.[44]

A popular way of securing prescription drugs is "doctor shopping." The doctor shopper visits multiple physicians claiming symptoms that might result in prescriptions for narcotic drugs like Percocet and OxyContin. A Florida man represents a typical case. Authorities were alerted when the man showed up at multiple pharmacies with prescriptions from different doctors. Subsequent investigation revealed the man had made 34 visits to 14 different doctors in a single 30-day period.[45] Doctor shoppers may be seeking the drugs for their own use or they may re-sell them in the illegal drug market. During my tenure with the

Cincinnati Vice Squad, we had several instances of men coercing female companions to function as doctor shoppers. In these particular cases, the women aroused fewer suspicions than their male partners. In some cases, the drugs fed the addiction of one or both of the couple involved but in others, the drugs were simply re-sold in the illegal market.

Use of fraudulent prescriptions is another diversion mechanism. Offenders may use stolen or forged prescription forms, alter legitimate prescriptions or impersonate physicians and phone in fake prescriptions for themselves or confederates. Watchful pharmacists constitute the main defense against this form of diversion.

One of the saddest aspects of the pharmaceutical diversion picture is the involvement of medical professionals. No professional group is immune to addictions and, occasionally, the high level of trust society places in health professionals, particularly physicians, enables their continuing addictive behavior. In the early 1980s I was involved in the start-up of a hospital based addictions treatment program. As we were seeking a medical director for the program, hospital personnel were adamant they had the perfect candidate and assigned a seemingly well-qualified physician to the position. As the new staff of the addictions program began to work together with the doctor, it became apparent that the newly assigned medical director himself had a pill and alcohol problem. The staff organized an intervention and the doctor agreed to enter treatment for his own addiction.

By the doctor's own account, he had been drunk on duty a number of times and had even operated on patients while intoxicated. Hospital staff members covered up for him, citing job stress and marital problems as the reasons behind his erratic behavior. In recovery, the doctor believed staff insistence that he was a good candidate for medical director of the addictions program was their way of indirectly confronting him. The good news is that he was successful in his treatment and rejoined the program as a medical consultant. He later became an articulate spokesperson on the issue of addictions among physicians and other medical professionals.

Addiction rates among medical people are similar to the rates for the general population, with alcohol the primary drug of choice. But programs that specialize in treating addictions are recording some change in the pattern. The Washington Physicians Health Program, a Washington State group, notes that "increasingly the drugs of choice are ones doctors can easily get their hands on—hydrocodone and oxycodone—powerful painkillers that can give the user a euphoric high."[46]

Addiction drives most of the medical diversion activity, but in a few cases, corrupt individuals use the drugs as a tool to coerce sex and money from their patients. In 2004, a Maryland dentist was arrested for writing false prescriptions for female patients. The dentist was trading prescriptions for OxyContin, Vicodin, and other drugs in return for sexual favors. He was arrested following an undercover operation.[47]

In a case in Hamilton, Ohio, which prosecutors referred to as "unique" and "bizarre," identical twin brothers, both respected pediatricians, were convicted of drug and child molestation charges. The brothers had for years been providing drugs to teenage boys in exchange for sexual acts. Their behavior came to light when one of their former patients, drug addicted and in a treatment program, reported his experience to authorities.[48]

The problem of prescription drug abuse is widespread. National surveys found over six million Americans reporting non-medical use of prescription drugs in the previous 30 days. This is a level of use that outstrips all other illegal drug use with the exception of marijuana.[49] Because prescription drug abuse covers multiple drug categories including pain relievers, stimulants and psychotherapeutics, the consequences of the abuse are varied as well. Among the prescription drugs used illegally, opioid pain relievers represent the most often abused, and addiction to these drugs is a significant risk.

Addiction to prescription medicine is by now a staple of the celebrity news world. Rush Limbaugh, Brett Favre, Robert Downey Jr., Chevy Chase, and Cindy McCain (wife of Senator John McCain) have all publically acknowledged their addiction to prescription drugs. Yet for the most part, non-celebrities addicted to pain medicines fly under the public radar. While those addicted to illegal drugs risk both arrest and violence in the street drug market, the pill addict is most-often supplied by doctors and pharmacists who are treating them for depression, pain problems, and a variety of other health complaints.

Non-medical use of pharmaceuticals is most common at both ends of the age spectrum. After marijuana use, prescription drug abuse constitutes the largest category of illegal drug use by young Americans. In 2008, 5.9% of those aged 18-25 reported current (previous 30 days) non-medical use of prescription drugs.[50] While the 2008 figures show a one-tenth of one-percent decline from 2007, the longer term trend is up. The 2008 figure represents an over 7% increase compared to 2002.[51]

Non-medical use of drugs by older Americans is also increasing. In fact, such use has increased dramatically over the past several years. For Americans aged 55-59, current non-medical use of prescription drugs jumped from 1.9% in 2002 to a reported 5% in 2008, a163% increase.[52] The participation of older Americans in the drug diversion picture is likely only to increase in the next decade. The level of drug diversion activity by Americans older than 60 is not even tracked by the government; but given the increase in the 50-59 age cohort, it is logical that the problem among those in their 60's and above is higher yet than those found in the younger age group. The unrestrained costs of healthcare and the aging of the American population virtually guarantee that the country will be facing a major age-related drug diversion problem over the coming years.

Complicating the control of drug diversion is the growing role of the Internet in prescription drug distribution. In Congressional Committee Hearings on the problem of drug diversion, Joshua Halpern, an executive with IntegriChain, an "internet threat management" firm, stated there are an estimated 3000 websites selling drugs directly to users.[53] Legally, these sites require that purchasers submit a prescription before forwarding the drugs, a requirement easily and commonly circumvented. The sheer volume of drug sellers available through the internet with many companies and websites located outside the United States make enforcement difficult. Richard M. Stana, a staffer with the U.S. Government Accountability Office, summarized the difficulties in controlling internet drug transactions. "It's very difficult for law enforcement to trace and do anything about the sale of the drugs by Internet sites," he said. "They're up for a while, they're down for a while. They change Web names, they change locations. It's just tough to get a handle on it."[54]

DISCUSSION

America's drug problem is more accurately described as a "drugs" problem. Our alcohol problem and our cocaine problem, while both major issues, represent radically different challenges. Tobacco causes more deaths than all the other drugs combined, yet because these deaths are in essence, slow motion, usually occurring after years of use, they lack the drama of an alcohol-related traffic death or the death of a teen from a heroin overdose.

Criminal violence related to drugs is a major concern. Despite the high level of violence that characterizes drug trafficking at every level, America's favorite drug, alcohol, remains the drug most likely to be associated with criminal violence. While alcohol may be numerically the drug most commonly associated with criminal violence, it is also by far the most widely used drug.

In contrast, the people using and trafficking in crack, heroin, and methamphetamine are involved in violence at a level that far outstrips their small percentage of the population. Further, due to its legal status, the proceeds from marketing alcohol are part of the legal economy and do not support the terrorism and violence that characterize the illegal drug market at the international and local levels.

Effective control of pharmaceutical diversion represents a difficult policy dilemma. Drug diversion covers such a wide variety of behaviors that crafting policy responses becomes correspondingly complicated. Much of the drug diversion activity is clearly criminal in nature; some of it is driven by addicts, the doctor shoppers being a prime example. Some of it is driven by organized crime groups which market stolen or counterfeit pills via the internet or street markets; and some of it results from petty criminality, teenagers sharing prescription meds at a "rave party," as an example.

Some drug diversion results from attempts to save money on prescription medication. The increasing Internet marketing of prescription drugs is in large measure driven by money issues. Drug diversion includes a husband with muscle aches who decides to take his wife's prescription pain pills to get some relief. And it includes the elderly couples who share each other's medication as a cost savings measure.

If we are to be successful in reducing drug problems, the policies and programs implemented will need to reflect the diversity of challenges that the various drugs present. Policy will need to be shaped more by factual information and less by emotion. The writer H.L. Mencken noted that for every complex problem, there is an answer that is both simple—And wrong. In no other public policy area do the lines seem so rigidly drawn. If we are to be more effective in responding to America's drug problem, the impulse to simple responses will need to be tempered and an openness to new approaches nurtured.

NOTES

1. Greater Dallas Area Council on Alcoholism and Drug Abuse. (2006). *Alcohol: Facts, statistics, resources and impairment charts.* Retrieved from http://www.gdcada.org/statistics/alcohol.htm.

2. Ibid.

3. Bureau of Justice Statistics (BJS). (1998). *Alcohol and Crime: An Analysis of National Data on the Prevalence of Alcohol Involvement in Crime.* Retrieved from http://www.ojp.usdoj.gov/bjs/pub/pdf/ac.pdf.

4. Ibid.

5. Harwood, H. (2000, December). *Updating Estimates of the Eco Economic Costs of Alcohol Abuse in the United States: Estimates, Update Methods, and Data.* Rockville, MD: National Institutes of Health.

6. National Institute on Drug Abuse (NIDA). (2006, July). "Tobacco Addiction." *NIDA Research Report Series, 06-4342.* Retrieved from http://www.nida.nih.gov/PDF/TobaccoRRS_v16.

7. Centers for Disease Control and Prevention (CDC). (1997, May 23). "Smoking-Attributable Mortality and Years of Potential Life Lost: United States, 1984." *Morbidity and Mortality Weekly Report, 46*(20). Retrieved from http://www.cdc.gov/mmwr/preview/mmwrhtml/00047690.

8. Ibid.

9. National Institute on Drug Abuse (NIDA). (2006, July). "Tobacco Addiction." *NIDA Research Report Series, 06-4342.* Retrieved from http://www.nida.nih.gov/PDF/TobaccoRRS_v16

10. Ibid.

11. Johnston, L.C., O'Malley, P.M., Bachman, J.G. & Schulenberg, J.E. (2007, December 11). "Overall, Illicit Drug Use by American Teens Continues Gradual Decline in 2007." *University of Michigan News Service: Ann Arbor.* Retrieved from *Monitoringthefuture*.org.

12. Ibid.

13. National Institute on Drug Abuse. (NIDA) (2005, July). "Marijuana Abuse." *NIDA Research Report Series, 05-3859.* Retrieved from http://www.drugabuse.gov/PDF/RRMarijuana.

14. National Institute on Drug Abuse. (NIDA) (2009, July). *NIDA Infofacts: Marijuana.* Retrieved from http://www.drugabuse.gov/infofacts/marijuana.html.

15. National Institute on Drug Abuse. (NIDA) (2005, July). "Marijuana Abuse." *NIDA Research Report Series, 05-3859.* Retrieved from http://www.drugabuse.gov/PDF/RRMarijuana.

16. Ibid.

17. Ibid.
18. Ibid.
19. Johnston, L.C., O'Malley, P.M., Bachman, J.G. & Schulenberg, J.E. (2007, December 11). "Overall, Illicit Drug Use by American Teens Continues Gradual Decline in 2007." *University of Michigan News Service: Ann Arbor.* Available from http://www.monitoringthefuture.org.
20. National Institute on Drug Abuse (NIDA) (2009, September) NIDA infofacts: Heroin {Data file}. Retrieved from http://www.nida.nih.gov/infofacts/heroin.html.
21. Ohio Resource Network for Safe and Drug Free Schools and Communities. (2006, May 26). "'Bad' Heroin Found After Epidemic of Overdoses." *Ohio Early Warning Alert.* Retrieved from http://www.ebasedprevention.org/files/ oewn/Heroin_Alert_ Supplement.pdf.
22. National Drug Intelligence Center (NDIC). (2006, June 5). *Fentanyl: Situation Report.* Retrieved from http://www.justice.gov/ndic/srs/20469/index.htm.
23. National Institute on Drug Abuse (NIDA) (2005, May). "Heroin Abuse and Addiction." *NIDA Research Report Series, 05-5165.* Retrieved from http://www.nida.nih. gov/PDF/RRHeroin.pdf.
24. Ibid.
25. Ibid.
26. National Institute on Drug Abuse (NIDA). (2004, November). "Cocaine Use and Addiction." *NIDA Research Report Series, 99-4342.* Retrieved from http://www.nida.nih.gov/PDF/RRCocaine.pdf.
27. Ibid.
28. Johnston, et al., "Illicit Drug Use by Teens Continues Decline."
29. NIDA, "Cocaine Use and Addiction."
30. Ibid.
31. Ibid.
32. Ibid.
33. Ibid.
34. Johnston, et al., "Illicit Drug Use by Teens Continues Decline."
35. National Institute on Drug Abuse (NIDA), (2006, September). Methamphetamine abuse and addiction, *NIDA Research Report Series,* 06-4210. Retrieved from http://www.nida.nih.gov/PDF/RRMetham.pdf.
36. Ibid.
37. Ibid.
38. Ibid.
39. Ibid.
40. SRNNews.com, (March 4 2011), "Drug Debate Apparent motive in Tacoma Homicide." Retrieved from http://srnnews.townhall.com/news/us/2011/03/04/drug_debate_apparent_motive_in_tacoma_homicide
41. Knickerbocker, B. (2005, July 15). "Meth's Rising U.S. Impact." *The Christian Science Monitor.* Retrieved from http://www.csmonitor.com/2005/0715/p03s01-ussc.html.
42. Ibid.
43. National Drug Intelligence Center (NDIC0) (2004, November) "Pharmaceuticals Drug Threat Assessment." Retrieved from http://www.justice.gov/ndic/pubs11/11449/diversion.htm
44. Ibid.
45. Ibid.

46. Jenkins, Austin (2009, January 22). "Federal Prosecutors Crack Down on Addicted Doctors." OPB News, Retrieved from http://www.justice.gov/ndic/pubs11/11449/diversion.htm.

47. National Drug Intelligence Center (NDIC) (2004, November) "Pharmaceuticals Drug Threat Assessment." Retrieved from http://www.justice.gov/ndic/pubs11/11449/diversion.htm.

48. Morse, Janet (2009, March 7). "Twin pediatricians face charges of molestation." Cincinnati Enquirer, Retrieved from http://www.enquirer.com/editions/pdf/KY_CE_070309.pdf

49. Substance Abuse and Mental health Services Administration. (2009) Results from the 2008 National Survey on Drug Use and Health: National Findings (Office of Applied Studies, NSDUH Series H-36, HHS Publication No. SMA 09-4434. Rockville, MD.

50. Ibid.

51. Ibid.

52. Ibid.

53. Thompson, Cheryl. (2009, January 15). "Internet Experts Testify About Illegal Drug Sales." *Pharmacy News*. Retrieved from http://www.ashp.org/menu/News/PharmacyNews/NewsArticle.aspx?id=2078.

54. Ibid.

Chapter 7

Addiction: The Driving Force behind the Illegal Drug Market

> *"Dope never helped anybody sing better or play music better or do anything better. All dope can do for you is kill you—and kill you the long, slow, hard way."*
>
> Billie Holiday
> (American jazz singer)

Given the wide recognition of the dangers associated with alcohol and drugs, it is logical to ask why so many Americans both use and abuse these substances.

There are a multitude of reasons given to explain drug use. Peer pressure, psychological problems, adolescent risk-taking, genetic predisposition, unemployment, physical problems, sexual inadequacy, boredom, seeking a religious experience—the list of reasons goes on and on. The motivations to use drugs are likely as varied as the individuals making the choice to use.

When I was a counselor in a drug treatment program in the 1970's, we once got into a group discussion of why the participants, all long term heroin addicts, used drugs. As we went around the group, the usual litany of reasons, "can't get a job, fight with the girlfriend, etc." were bantered about. Finally, one of the newer women in the group, who had not yet caught onto the correct things to say in group therapy, retorted, "You all are crazy. All I want to do is rest up a bit and then get back out there and get high!"

Everybody laughed but the point was well made. Wanting to feel good, to experience pleasure, is a basic human behavior. All of us are looking for a pleasurable experience and human beings have used drugs to that end for thousands of years.

While drug use clearly underlies major social problems, the fact remains that the overwhelming majority of people who use drugs do so without that use causing them significant problems. But for a minority of the people using drugs, the use escalates and results in substantial life problems, a state of affairs generally described as drug addiction. Addiction is more than a pharmacological equation. It involves the personal characteristics of the individual, as well as a complex interplay of environmental factors. Research on alcoholism, perhaps the oldest of the addiction problems, increasingly points to a genetic link for alcoholism and perhaps other drug addictions as well.[1]

The concept of addiction itself is difficult to describe. People involved in research on or treatment of drug problems make careful distinctions in describing physical dependence, psychological dependence, addiction, and other related terms. In the methadone program where I worked early in my career, we operated under strict federal guidelines which limited participation to those who were physically addicted—defined as being a user for significant period of time and an individual who would experience withdrawal symptoms if deprived of heroin. Heroin withdrawal was considered especially horrific and the general belief was that addicts facing withdrawal would do almost anything to "get well," that is, get some heroin. This perception of heroin addiction and withdrawal was fed by media portrayals of heroin users, particularly a popular 1955 movie, *The Man with the Golden Arm.* The film starred Frank Sinatra as Frankie Machine, a heroin addict, and included scenes of Sinatra writhing in agony as he attempted to quit cold turkey on his heroin addiction. I was somewhat astounded to be told by the recovering heroin addicts I worked with that heroin withdrawal was actually somewhat similar to a case of the flu—very unpleasant but not even close to the excruciating experience Sinatra portrayed.

Experts quarrel over a precise definition of addiction. Years ago, addiction was a term that included two components—tolerance to the drug and physical symptoms on withdrawal of the drug. There was argument over whether a particular drug caused physical dependence versus psychological dependence. In this view, the more dangerous or addictive drugs, heroin being the prime example, represented true physical dependence. In the 1970s, cocaine was viewed as a much less dangerous drug than heroin. In fact, among the treatment staff at the methadone program where I worked, a positive urine for cocaine in the absence of heroin was viewed as a small success. Alcohol was seen as an entirely separate issue. When clients scheduled for a urine test were unable to perform, they were sometimes sent to the bar next door for a beer or two to speed up the process. Modern treatment professionals are no doubt horrified to learn this, yet, in the 1970s, it was state of the art.

Alcoholism counselors of that era viewed their clients' problems differently than professionals in drug addiction treatment. Rather than focusing on the physical effects of the drug (alcohol), they focused on the person. An alcoholic was a person who had lost control over drinking to the extent it was causing problems in his or her life. A slogan frequently heard from Alcoholism Counselors was "if alcohol causes problems, it is the problem." Drug professionals tended to see the addict's life problems as the root of the addiction and focused their efforts on improving psychological and social functioning believing that with improvement, the drug problem would go away. Alcoholism people focused on the drug. Quit drinking, one day at a time, and the related life problems will improve.

The current view of drug addiction has moved from an emphasis on the physical and psychological impact of the drug to emphasis on the impact of the drug use on the user's life. This emphasis is at the core of the definition of addiction now used by the National Institute of Drug Abuse (NIDA). As expressed by Dr. Alan Lershner, director of NIDA:

> What does matter tremendously is whether or not a drug causes what we now know to be the essence of addiction: *uncontrollable, compulsive drug seeking and use, even in the face of negative health and social consequences.* This is the crux of how many professional organizations all define addiction, and how we all should use the term. It is really only this expression of addiction - *uncontrollable, compulsive craving, seeking and use of drugs* - that matters to the addict and to his or her family, and that should matter to society as a whole. These are the elements responsible for the massive health and social problems caused by drug addiction [emphasis in the original].[2]

There is also increasing recognition that the pharmaceutical effects of the drug are only a part of the addiction picture. In the 1970s, it was popularly believed that one use of heroin would start a person down the road to addiction. The experience of veterans who used heroin in Vietnam shattered that belief.

In 1971, heroin use was prevalent among enlisted men in Vietnam. The concern was that their heroin addiction would continue with their return to civilian life and the country would be facing a massive heroin addiction problem. This concern generated government sponsored research on the issue, with some surprising outcomes.

> *Drug Dealing—A Risky Business*
> Prince George's County police have identified the man slain yesterday in his Adelphi home as 22-year-old Justin Vance Desha-Overcash. Police said they recovered marijuana, a digital scale and drug packaging materials from the home, indicating the Desha-Overcash was selling drugs. Police have not identified a suspect in the killing.[3]

Researchers uncovered two important findings. The first was the use of narcotics was much more common than previously estimated with 43% of the soldiers reporting heroin and/or opium use. Using military records and reports from the men themselves, researchers judged that 20% of the soldiers using these drugs had an addiction to narcotics while in Vietnam.[4]

The second finding was even more startling. All soldiers with a record of addiction were detoxified on their return from Vietnam. They were then followed through their return to civilian life. Only a small number, 12% of those described as addicted while in Vietnam, were addicted during the year after their return to civilian life. This rate of addiction was no different than the addiction of rate of men who had not served in the military.[5]

In a different fashion, the public view of cocaine underwent an interesting metamorphosis in the 1980s. In 1986, the perception that cocaine was a relatively harmless drug was turned upside down with the death of Len Bias. Bias was a star basketball player at the University of Maryland. In June of 1986, he became the first round draft choice of the Boston Celtics. Two days later, Bias was found dead in his dorm room, a victim of a cocaine overdose. The shock of Bias's death intensified eight days later with the cocaine related death of Don Rogers. Rogers was a Cleveland Browns defensive back and one of the rising stars in the NFL. Rogers had been a first round draft pick of the Browns and had been named rookie of the year in 1985.

The cocaine deaths of Bias and Rogers, star athletes in the prime of their careers, helped to create the perception of cocaine as a powerful, highly addictive drug. Media coverage of the emergence of crack cocaine in the inner cities escalated with the theme that crack, powerful and cheap, was sweeping across the country. An article in the in September 21, 1986, L.A. Times claimed, "the processing of crystallized cocaine as 'rock' or 'crack' has so lowered the price—and increased the availability—that junior high school students are pooling their lunch money... to buy cocaine from schoolyard dealers."[6]

Babies born to crack-addicted women were a central focus of the media coverage in the mid to late 1980s. In a July 1986 story on the drug crisis, headlined "Cocaine Babies: Hooked at Birth," Newsweek Magazine reported on the problems of what would widely be described as "crack babies." The story reported on two specific infants:

> Guillermo, a newborn at Broward General Medical Center in Ft. Lauderdale, has spent his whole short life crying. He is jittery and goes into spasms when he is touched. His eyes don't focus. He can't stick out his tongue, or suck. Born a week ago to a cocaine addict, Guillermo is described by his doctors as an addict himself. Nearby, a baby named Paul lies motionless in an incubator, feeding tubes riddling his tiny body. He needs a respirator to breathe and a daily spinal tap to relieve fluid buildup on his brain. Only one month old, he has already suffered two strokes.[7]

The "crack baby" caricature was myth. Deborah Frank, a professor of Pediatrics at Boston University, later described the "crack baby" as "a grotesque media stereotype [and] not a scientific diagnosis."[8] She found that in pregnant crack users the drug's impact on the fetus is similar to the negative effects of tobacco or alcohol use, poor prenatal care or poor nutrition.

The incredible addictive power of cocaine was widely accepted. In the late 1980s, I attended three different drug conferences where speakers repeated the same findings of recent animal research on cocaine addiction. The research, as presented to the crowds of drug treatment professionals, involved laboratory rats conditioned to press a bar in their cage to bring a food pellet. Once the behavior was established, the researchers then stopped the food pellets and counted how many bar presses the rats would make before giving up, or in research terms, the behavior was "extinguished." On average, the speakers reported, the rats would press the bar 150 times with no food before giving up.

The researchers then placed tiny electrodes on the brains of the rats and with each press of the bar, the rat would be given a sexual orgasm. As with the food, the orgasms were then stopped, yet the rats continued to press the bar on average 500 times before giving up. No one was particularly surprised to learn orgasms were more powerful reinforcement than food pellets.

The researchers then rewired the rats so that with a press of the bar, they would receive a small hit of cocaine. The cocaine was then withdrawn and researchers watched the rats continue to press the bar hoping for cocaine. In their attempts to get more cocaine, the speakers told us the rats continued to press the bar on average 1500 times before giving up. The message was clear! This stuff was more powerful, more pleasurable than sex. No one, including myself, challenged the purported finding. In fact, I am sure a significant percentage of the audience was considering getting some cocaine in anticipation of the intense euphoric experience promised.

Months later, I repeated this story to a friend of mine, a biologist working in animal research. After a period of laughter, he advised rats did not experience the human equivalent of orgasms. However, the willingness of me and other audience members to believe this exaggerated picture of the addictive power of cocaine was evidence of the influence of the hyperbolic media coverage of the drug.

There has been a volume of animal research related to drugs. In fact, Morgan and Zimmer wryly note, "Laboratory scientists sometimes joke that the definition of a drug is any substance that, when injected into a rat, produces a journal article."[9] In fairness, there were a number of animal studies that seemed to document the fact that cocaine was highly addictive, yet whether these findings were applicable to human populations was uncertain. However, an extensive review of the animal research and a direct comparison to human drug taking behavior led to a somewhat shocking conclusion. Researchers Peele and DeGrandpre found a surprising congruence between animal and human behavior. "Actually, despite claims to the contrary, there is no disagreement between animal models of drug taking and naturalistic drug use: in both spheres all drug use depends on individual history and prevailing environmental circumstances."[10]

Studies of human beings using cocaine found results that somewhat echo the heroin research on Vietnam veterans. In a 1985 study of those who reported use of cocaine, the majority of users, about half the males and two-thirds of the females, had used less than 10 times in their lifetime. Roughly a third of both males and females reported lifetime use of 10 to 99 times. Nine percent of the males and three percent of the females reported use between 100 and 999 times, and 3% of the males and 2% of the females reported lifetime use of over 1,000 times.[11]

Other studies document similar findings of a small percentage of users identified as heavy users. A Canadian survey found only five percent of people describing themselves as current users who used cocaine on a monthly or more basis.[12] Another study found approximately 10% to 25% of regular cocaine users took the drug in a fashion that fits the clinical description of addition.[13]

While studies of illegal behavior like drug taking always bring some questions on validity, it seems fair to say that a small number of people consume most of the cocaine used. This pattern of heavy users, people we would likely describe as addicts, accounting for a high percentage of the overall drug consumption, likely extends to other drug categories, including alcohol.

DISCUSSION

Drug addiction is a complex phenomenon with elements that include the pharmacologic characteristics of the drug used, the physiological and psychological traits of the individual using, and the environment surrounding the drug and the user. Despite this complexity, there are reasonable assumptions we can make that clarify the role of addiction in the overall drug picture.

- *The large majority of people who use any drug will use it without causing serious problems for themselves or others.* The idea that any use of a drug is the first step toward an inevitable addiction is false. Non-addicted users will sometimes cause problems—driving under the influence, accidental overdoses, and disorderly behavior under the influence are examples. However, the majority of these people will engage in occasional drug use in a fashion similar to what we would describe as social use of alcohol.

- *A minority of users will use in the compulsive fashion we would describe as addiction.* This addictive use will cause them significant life problems. For this group, their drug seeking and/or behavior under the influence will bring them into the health care, social services, and criminal justice systems. The problems their addiction generates will directly and significantly impact their families, employers, schools, and the community at large.

- *Addicted users account for the majority of the demand for drugs. It is addicted users that sustain the illegal drug trade.* Without these high level drug consumers, the demand for drugs would significantly decrease. While the exact role in terms of drug quantity these users represent is difficult to estimate and likely varies by geographic location and drug category, it is a reasonable assumption that addicted users account for at least half of the country's total drug consumption.

Any strategy to reduce drug consumption must address these heavy users.

- *Addiction treatment is effective and provides hope to even the most desperate of addicted people.* The literature on effectiveness of drug treatment (See NIDA and NIAAA websites) is persuasive. I currently volunteer in the *Off the Streets* program, an effort to assist women trying to leave street prostitution. Addiction is a problem for virtually all of these women. Most treatment professionals would view them as poor candidates for long term success. Yet we see women with the most horrendous histories overcome their addiction and lead sober and successful lives.

Understanding the role of addiction in the country's drug problem is critical to effectively addressing it. Much of our current approach does not discriminate between users who pose no serious problem to themselves or others and addicted users who constitute the bulk of the demand that fuels the drug market. An approach that directs enforcement, legal and social services resources toward these high level users of drugs will show more success than the current approach.

NOTES

1. Dick, Danielle and Agrawal, Arpana (2008). "The Genetics of Alcohol and Other Drug Dependence." Alcohol Research & Health, Vol. 31, No. 2. P. 111, National Institute on Alcohol Abuse and Alcoholism (NIAAA).
2. Lershner, A. (2001, March). The Essence of Drug Addiction. *National Institute of Drug Abuse.* Retrieved from http://www.drugabuse.gov/Published_Articles/Essence.html.
3. (Zapotosky, White and Klein (2011, February). "Portraits of the 16 Killed This Year in Prince George's County." *Washington Post.*
4. Robins, L.N., Davis, D.H. & Nurco, D.N..(1974). "How Permanent Was Vietnam Drug Addiction?" *American Journal of Public Health, 64* (Suppl), 38-43.
5. Robins, L.N., Helzer, J.E., Hesselbrock., M & Wish, E. (1980). "Vietnam Veterans Three Years After Vietnam: How Our Study Changed Our View Of Heroin." In L. Brill & C. Winick (Eds.). *Yearbook of Substance Use and Abuse.* New York: Human Science Press.
6. Montague, P (Ed.). "America's Secret Drug War." *Third World Traveler.* Retrieved from http://www.thirdworldtraveler.com/CIA/secret_war.html.
7. Barol, B. Prout, L. Fitzgerald, K., Katz, S. & King, P. (1986, July 28). "Cocaine Babies: Hooked at Birth." *Newsweek,* 56.
8. Frank, Deborah, M.D. (2002) Testimony before the United States Sentencing Commission. February 21, 2002.
9. Morgan, J. P. & Zimmer, L. (1997). "The Social Pharmacology of Smokeable Cocaine: Not All It's Cracked Up to Be." In. C. Reinarman and H. Levine (Eds.). *Crack in America: Demon Drugs and Social Justice.* Regents of the University of California.

10. Peele, Stanton & DeGrandpre, Richard. (1998). Cocaine and the Concept of Addiction: Environmental Factors in Drug Compulsions." Addiction Research, Retrieved from http://www.peele.net/lib/cocaine.html.

11. Kandel, D. B., Murphy, D., & Karus, D. (1985). "Cocaine Use in Young Adulthood: Patterns of Use and Psychosocial Correlates." In N. J. Kozel and E. H. Adams (Eds.). *Cocaine Use in America: Epidemiologic and Clinical Perspectives.* Washington, DC: U.S. Government Printing Office: 76-110.

12. Adlaf, E. M., Smart, R. G., & Canale, M. D. (1991). *Drug Use among Ontario Adults 1977-1991.* Toronto: Ontario Addiction Research Foundation.

13. Erickson, P. G., & Alexander, B. K. (1989). Cocaine and addictive liability. *Social Pharmacology, 3*, 249-270.

Chapter 8

Marijuana—The Cartel's Cash Cow

> *"When I was in England, I experimented with marijuana a time or two, and I didn't like it, and I didn't inhale, and I never tried it again."*
>
> Bill Clinton
March 29, 1992

> *"When I was a kid I inhaled frequently. That was the point."*
>
> Barack Obama
November 4, 2003

As marijuana is the most used illegal drug in the United States, policy changes related to marijuana have the potential to significantly undercut the illegal market. Much of the discussion revolves around two simple proposals—one to legalize marijuana and one to tax it. The "legalize it" argument generally assumes legalization as an "either/or" proposition. However, if the federal government were to take action to end national marijuana prohibition, under the 10th Amendment to the U.S. Constitution (1), the responsibility for marijuana policy would revert to the states.

The situation is analogous to the end of alcohol prohibition. With the repeal of the Volstead Act, the national alcohol prohibition experiment was over. Each state was free to deal with alcohol as it decided. The result was a wide range of diverse regulations. States created a myriad of systems of Alcohol Beverage Control (ABC) laws that included licensing systems for alcohol outlets, hours of sale regulations, drinking age restrictions, and limits on the number of alcohol outlets per geographic area. Some states allowed local jurisdictions to impose their own regulations and a large number of jurisdictions decided to remain "dry," maintaining some form of alcohol prohibition. This variety of alcohol regulation from jurisdiction to jurisdiction continues to this day.[1]

It is reasonable to presume that states would adopt a similar variety of strategies at the end of marijuana prohibition. Some states would move to legalize marijuana and develop the necessary regulatory controls. Other states might choose to maintain marijuana prohibition and keep some criminal sanctions in place. In short, marijuana policy would begin to resemble the current alcohol control system with a variety of regulations reflecting the values and sentiments of the local population.

In considering the end of marijuana prohibition, the end of the alcohol prohibition experiment provides some direction. The circumstances surrounding marijuana today are similar to those at the end of alcohol prohibition. Analogous to alcohol at the end of prohibition, marijuana is used by a significant percentage of the population. According to the 2009 federal survey of drug use, over 25 million Americans aged 12 and older used marijuana in the past year.[2] Over the last several years, many Americans have become increasingly tolerant of marijuana use and have supported a variety of legislative initiatives liberalizing marijuana laws.

As an example, in 2004, Oakland (CA) voters supported a measure which directs the Oakland Police Department to make marijuana enforcement the city's "lowest law enforcement priority."[3] The measure passed by a 64% to 36% margin. In 2006, voters in Santa Barbara, California approved a similar measure, which has since withstood a legal challenge.[4] A number of states have passed laws making marijuana possession an offense that allows for a citation to court rather than a physical arrest and fifteen states now have passed medical marijuana laws. In 2009, voters in Breckenridge, Colorado, voted by a 3 to 1 margin to legalize marijuana in their jurisdiction.[5]

Marijuana advocates are also directly challenging marijuana-related penalties on college campuses, claiming the stiff punishment meted out to offenders is partly to blame for alcohol problems on campuses. A Denver-based group, Safer Alternatives for Enjoyable Recreation, argues that marijuana-related penalties drive students to abuse alcohol, leading to binge drinking and other problems. The group supports equalizing the penalties that students face for marijuana and alcohol offenses. Mike Tvert, spokesperson for the group, has organized votes on the issue at 13 colleges and students have voted in favor at each campus.[6]

Changing social attitudes toward marijuana have even reached perhaps the most conservative element in the country, the law enforcement community. The majority of law enforcement agencies now accept applicants who have used marijuana. The Federal Bureau of Investigation (FBI) has a typical policy. Applicants to the FBI who have used marijuana are now considered for agent positions if they have not used within the three years prior to their application.[7]

The "tax it" piece of the argument assumes a significant windfall of tax dollars following legalization. Again, the current situation is similar to that surrounding alcohol when national prohibition was repealed in 1933. At that time, the country was in the grips of The Great Depression, and the promise of jobs and tax revenue for governments as a result of legalization was a powerful argument for repeal.[8]

The amount of tax revenue that could be generated through legal marijuana is difficult to estimate and would largely depend on how the taxes would be structured. Despite this, there is little doubt, given the widespread use of marijuana, that the potential for tax income is significant. Researcher John Gettman, assuming marijuana taxes as a percentage of the total business in the same fashion as legitimate corporations, estimates potential tax revenue nationally of over $15 billion.[9] An estimate of the potential tax revenue related to a legalization bill in California projected $1.4 billion for the state, an estimate described as conservative.[10] The $15 billion estimate assumes national legalization of marijuana rather than the state by state piecemeal approach more likely to occur.

Marijuana legalization continues to be vociferously debated. The precise consequences of moving marijuana from a prohibition context to a legal-regulatory system are unknown. Many of the arguments on both sides are based more on emotion than logic but an objective review of some of the arguments can put the marijuana legalization debate into a more rational framework. A brief overview of some of the major points of contention follows.

MARIJUANA AS HARMLESS VERSUS MARIJUANA AS A DANGEROUS DRUG

In fact, marijuana is neither the benevolent weed the stoner community worships nor is it the devil weed so feared by marijuana prohibitionists. From a public health perspective, smoking marijuana carries with it similar and perhaps somewhat heightened risks compared to those associated with tobacco.[11] Yet the overdose risk and the risk of addiction are significantly lower than other commonly abused drugs, including alcohol. The addictive potential of marijuana is low, with some researchers ranking it below caffeine.[12] Further, overdose deaths from marijuana are virtually unheard of and aspirin is considered a more significant overdose risk than marijuana.[13]

Prohibitionists note that the potency of marijuana has increased over the past years and that smoking marijuana exposes users to the unknown risks of ingesting the many other unknown substances commonly found in illegal marijuana. Yet these are two issues that could be effectively addressed within a legalization framework. Regulatory standards would control product quality and standards mandating limits on the potency of legal marijuana could be imposed similar to those controlling the alcohol content in beer, wine, and liquor.

LEGALIZATION WOULD MEAN MORE USERS AND MARIJUANA RELATED SOCIAL PROBLEMS VERSUS FEWER

The question is twofold. First, if marijuana were to become available via legal means, would that mean more users? And second, if there are new users, what sort of additional social problems would more users create?

Legalization advocates claim in the long run, less pot use might result, particularly among teens, and point to Holland as evidence for their position. In Holland, where marijuana is not legal but possession for personal use is allowed, 28% of high school sophomores report using marijuana compared to 41% of American sophomores.[14] LEAP also notes that the University of Michigan survey of high school students found nearly 90% reporting it was easy or fairly easy to buy drugs and LEAP suggests that drugs might be more difficult to obtain under a legal framework.[15]

Prohibitionists believe legalization would encourage new users. Mark Davis, a Dallas radio commentator, makes the argument that laws do prevent people from using drugs and that legalization would certainly result in an increase in drug users:

> When a teenager is offered a handful of pills and says no out of fear of arrest, our drug laws work. When an adult refuses a joint at a party for fear of being busted on the way home, our drug laws work. Millions of Americans refrain from dabbling in drugs only because they are law-abiding and do not wish to go to jail. Lift those constraints, and you will see new experimentation at every age level.[16]

If you believe that the number of marijuana users would increase under a legalization framework, the second of our questions is whether the "new experimentation," as Davis puts it, will result in more social problems.

While no one can predict with certainty, it seems logical to assume there will be more users, at least temporarily, as those who have been constrained by legal barriers decide to try marijuana. It is also logical to presume that a small portion of those users will develop problems related to their marijuana use. This change would have to be balanced against the current costs of criminalizing millions of marijuana users as well as the economic benefits of generating significant tax revenue from legal marijuana.

LEGALIZATION LEADING TO MORE CRIME AND VIOLENCE VERSUS LEGALIZATION LEADING TO LESS CRIME AND VIOLENCE

Prohibition advocates argue that "crime, violence and drug use go hand in hand. Six times as many homicides are committed by people under the influence of drugs, as by those who are looking for money to buy drugs. Most drug crimes aren't committed by people trying to pay for drugs; they're committed by people on drugs."[17] This is an argument made in general about drug legalization that does not stand up when specifically applied to marijuana. While the behavior of individuals under the influence of marijuana varies, violent behavior is not generally associated with marijuana use. In fact, the *Marijuana Abuse Research Report,* produced by the federal government, does not even mention violence.[18]

In my experience as a police officer, the primary risk in use of marijuana involves the purchase of the drug in the illegal market. People seeking to buy marijuana may end up as victims of assault, robbery and rape. Most of the assaults and robberies around drug markets are what cops refer to as "a drug deal gone bad" and individuals trying to purchase marijuana are viewed as prime targets for violence. Buying marijuana in illegal markets is a risky proposition that brings the user into contact with drug dealers, whose daily existence is dependent on their willingness and ability to use violence. It also brings them access to cocaine, heroin and other illegal drugs, thus facilitating the use of those drugs as well. Moving marijuana to a legal market would largely eliminate the criminal connection between users and sellers, reducing violence and making the purchase of other drugs more difficult. This "separation of markets" is a primary element in the Dutch Drug Policy and may be worth implementing in the United States.

> *Chicago Slayings Drug-Related*
>
> A Chicago man recently convicted of weapons crimes was charged in the drug-related slayings of three men whose bodies were found inside an abandoned car last year on the Southwest Side, authorities said. Roberto Cerda, 24, of the 5600 block of South Trumbull Avenue, was charged Wednesday night with first-degree murder in the slayings of Andres Butron, 34, Ernesto Alequin, 42, and Hector Romero, 28, whose bodies were discovered in May 2010 near 48th Place and Whipple Street.[19]

ALCOHOL CAUSES TREMENDOUS PROBLEMS WHICH MARIJUANA WOULD MAKE WORSE

The fact is that alcohol does cause numerous problems. Prohibitionist supporters see marijuana legalization as a recipe for a worsening of those problems, particularly impaired driving: The DEA argues:

> Drunk driving is one of the primary killers of Americans. Do we want our bus drivers, nurses, and airline pilots to be able to take drugs one evening, and operate freely at work the next day? Do we want to add to the destruction by making drugged driving another primary killer?[20]

The impact of marijuana legalization on impaired driving is difficult to predict. Marijuana use clearly impairs driving skills. Currently, six to eleven percent of traffic fatalities are positive for marijuana. Research by the National Highway Traffic Safety Administration found moderate doses of marijuana impairing driving skills, and using alcohol in conjunction with marijuana led to a level of impairment greater than the sole use of alcohol or marijuana.[21] Whether legalization would create an increase beyond the six to eleven percent currently estimated is impossible to determine. Current OVI (Operating a Vehicle Under the Influence) laws cover drugged driving and testing technology to identify marijuana impairment is available. The issue is whether any increase in drugged driving, if it in fact occurs, would be offset by gains in other areas.

The arguments for and against legalization are familiar and have been debated extensively. To make a policy judgment on these arguments, the criteria of effectiveness, fairness, and cost benefit as outlined previously provides a reasonable basis for the decision.

On effectiveness, only the most determined optimist can view the results over the last thirty years and call the policy effort against marijuana a success. The youth use pattern as tracked by the University of Michigan annual survey shows relatively little long-term change. In fact, the most current data show a sharp increase in overall marijuana use nationally in 2009 and the potency of marijuana has increased over the years.[22] In addition, Americans have demonstrated an increasing tolerance for marijuana use. Medical marijuana legislation has passed in fifteen states, and a large number of local and state laws have defined marijuana possession as a minor misdemeanor offense handled in the same fashion as a traffic ticket. The current prohibition strategy continues to criminalize the twenty-five million Americans who have used marijuana, diverts scarce criminal justice resources from other drug and criminal problems needing more attention and provides billions of dollars to criminal organizations that are now directly threatening our national borders.

On the fairness issue, the weight of the argument goes against the prohibitionists. Given the millions of Americans from all walks of life who have used marijuana, this means that for each person arrested for marijuana, the odds are good that the police officer who made the arrest, the prosecutor who argued the case, and the judge who handed down the sentence or all the above, have themselves used marijuana. Public officials who have publicly acknowledged their past marijuana use include presidents, mayors, governors, senators and Supreme Court Justices. A partial list includes Barrack Obama, Bill Clinton, Al Gore, Newt Gingrich, Arnold Schwarzenegger, John Kerry, David Patterson, Howard Dean, John Edwards, Michael Bloomberg, Clarence Thomas and Douglas Ginsberg. In some cases the marijuana admission was hedged, usually described as youthful experimentation. However, Michael Bloomberg, the Mayor of New York, was refreshingly honest. When asked by a reporter if he had ever smoked marijuana, Bloomberg replied, "You bet I did and I enjoyed it."[23]

Criminalizing the use of marijuana in the face of its use by social elites represents the height of hypocrisy. A drug conviction carries lasting consequences beyond the criminal penalties imposed. It affects future employment, student loan eligibility, public housing access, and much more. To criminalize and impose punitive sanctions on behavior indulged in by the country's highest officials surely flunks the fairness test.

The cost benefit issue is perhaps the most persuasive argument for legalization. To get a sense of the potential financial impact of marijuana legalization, it is again useful to visit the alcohol prohibition experience. Historian Andrew Sinclair noted that prohibition transferred two billion dollars per year from legitimate businesses into the hands of "murderers" and "crooks."[24] Legalization of marijuana today would have the impact of transferring billions of dollars out of the hands of the murderers running drug cartels into the hands of the legal economy—farmers, corporations and the wholesale and retail network distributing the product.

The impact on farming alone would be significant. Marijuana is estimated to be the largest cash crop in the United States, with a total estimated value of $35.8 billion. The marijuana crop is worth more than all the corn and wheat crops combined. In twelve different states, marijuana is the number one cash crop and ranks as one of the top five cash crops in 39 states. Marijuana is bigger than cotton in Alabama, peanuts in Georgia and tobacco in South Carolina.[25] The movement of these dollars from the underground economy to the legal market would provide legitimate employment and sorely needed tax revenue.

Legalization would, of course, involve expenses. Regulatory agencies, along the lines of state alcohol authorities, would have to be established in those states where citizens choose the legalization option. At the federal level, regulation imposing manufacturing, product quality, and packaging standards would need to be developed and monitored. Taxing options at the federal, state and local level would all need to be developed with staffing for collection, auditing, inspection and enforcement required. This is a process the country has once before completed with the end of alcohol prohibition.

Savings in criminal justice spending related to marijuana enforcement could be redirected to other criminal justice or community priorities. There are a number of other financial implications that would spring from marijuana legalization. Potential additional health care costs, increased enforcement efforts to prevent drug impaired driving, and increased prevention programming might all be part of a changed policy landscape.

DISCUSSION

There is no rational reason to maintain the current prohibition approach to marijuana. Failure to directly address the issue has led to a disjointed system of control that largely relies on criminalizing the over 40% of Americans that have used marijuana. In large portions of the country, marijuana use and possession is now de facto legal, with penalties equivalent to traffic tickets. While this de facto legalization represents an improvement over the punitive prohibition approach, the failure to move marijuana into a legal regulatory control system leaves a "gray market" for pot that creates a new set of problems. It also fails to capitalize on the potential tax revenue inherent in legalization.

The prohibition approach has been clearly ineffective. It wastes resources that could be more effectively utilized, but even worse, prohibition has been clearly ineffective. Usage patterns are little changed, the potency of marijuana has increased over the years, and use of marijuana by the country's most visible leaders makes a mockery of the prohibition law. By moving marijuana from a prohibition context to a regulatory control system, we can show that the lessons of alcohol prohibition have finally been learned.

Most importantly, legalizing marijuana would begin to hamper the flood of money supporting drug traffickers. Legalization would end a significant percentage of the revenue flow of the major DTO's (Drug Trafficking Organizations). While domestic marijuana production is significant, marijuana smuggled into the country from Mexico remains the primary source of income to drug traffickers.[26] According to the National Drug Intelligence Report of 2007, "Despite the high level of domestic marijuana production by indoor and outdoor cannabis cultivators, marijuana flow from Mexico has remained high and possibly increased in 2007."[27]

Drug intelligence studies indicate that the amount of marijuana produced in Mexico, primarily for the U.S. market, is around 15,500 metric tons, an astonishing 34,177,500 pounds of marijuana.[28] Marijuana represents an income of $8.6 billion annually to Mexican cartels, an estimated 60% of the traffickers' total revenue.[29] Legalization could serve to divert those funds away from the DTO's into legitimate businesses and deprive traffickers of the revenue that supports their illegal and terrorist activities.

*The 10th Amendment reads, "The powers not delegated to the United States by the Constitution, nor prohibited by it to the States, are reserved to the States respectively, or to the people."

NOTES

1. Wikepedia (2009). "Alcohol laws of the United States." http://en.wikipedia.org/wiki/Alcohol_laws_of_the_United_States_by_state_
2. NSDUH (2009). National Survey on Drug Use and Health. Table 3G. Retrieved from http://www.oas.samhsa.gov/.
3. Stroup, Keith. (2004) "Drug War Briefs: Voters Nationwide Embrace Marijuana Law Reform Proposals." National Organization For Reform of Marijuana Laws (NORML). December 1, 2004.
4. Associated Press, (2007). "Santa Barbara Loses Legal Effort To Dump Pot Law." July 10, 2007.
5. TheDenverChannel.Com (2009). "Breckenridge Votes To Legalize Marijuana." http://www.thedenverchannel.com/news/21515178/detail.html. Retrieved 11/4/2009.
6. Callahan, Rick. (2009). "Colleges Urged To Mellow On Pot." Cincinnati Enquirer (AP), p. A9. May 17, 2009.
7. FBI (2009). Special Agent Frequently Asked Questions. http://www.fbi-jobs.gov/114.asp. Downloaded May 9, 2009.

8. Rickard, Earl (2001). "How Dry We Were: The Repeal of Prohibition." Retrieved from http://www.november.org/Prohibition/.
9. Gettman, John. (2007) "Lost Taxes and Other Costs of Marijuana Laws." The Bulletin of Cannabis Reform. www.Drugscience.org, downloaded May 11, 2009.
10. Parloff, Roger. (2009). "How Marijuana Became Legal." Fortune Magazine, September 18, 2009. On-line edition, http://rss.cnn.com/rss/magazines_fortune.rss. Retrieved November2, 2009.
11. NIDA (2005). Marijuana Abuse: NIDA Research Report Series, 05-3859. Retrieved from http://www.drugabuse.gov/PDF/RRMarijuana.pdf.
12. Schaefer, Clifford. (2009) "Basic Facts about the War on Drugs." http://www.druglibrary.org/schaffer/library/basicfax.htm. Downloaded May 13, 2009.
13. Ibid.
14. LEAP (2009). "End Prohibition Now!" Retrieved from http://www.leap.cc/read-discuss/publications/.
15. Ibid.
16. Davis, Mark. (2008) "Buckley, Legal Drugs and My Evolving View." Dallas Morning News. March 12, 2008.
17. DEA (2003, May). "Speaking Out Against Drug Legalization," U.S. Department of Justice, Drug Enforcement Administration.
18. NIDA, 2005.
19. Gorner, Jeremy (2009, June2). "No bail in slayings of 3 found in car." Chicago Tribune Online. Retrieved from http://articles.chicagobreakingnews.com/2011-06-02/news/29614708_1_drug-trafficking-crew-segura-rodriguez-and-augustin-toscano-slayings\.
20. DEA, 2003.
21. NIDA, 2005.
22. USA Today (2010). "Illegal Drug Use Up Sharply." USA Today. September 14, 2010.
23. Stenihauer, Jennifer. (2002) "Bloomberg Says He Regrets Marijuana Remarks." N.Y. Times. On-line Edition, April 10, 2002.
24. Sinclair, Andrew (1964). Era of excess: A social history of the prohibition movement. New York, NY: Harper and Row.
25. Gettman, "Lost Taxes and Other Costs of Marijuana Laws."
26. DOJ (2009). "National Drug Threat Assessment." National Drug Intelligence Center.
27. Ibid, 17.
28. Ibid, 19, 22.
29. Fainaru, Steve, and William Booth. (2009) "Cartels Face an Economic Battle." Washington Post, October 7, 2009. http://www.washingtonpost.com/wp-dyn/content/article/2009/10/06/AR2009100603847.html.Retrieved 10/30/2009.

Chapter 9

From Trafficking to Treatment

> *"It is our judgment that the war on drugs has failed, that it is diverting intelligent energy away from how to deal with the problem of addiction, that it is wasting our resources, and that it is encouraging civil, judicial, and penal procedures associated with police states."*
>
> National Review
> July 1, 1996

The policy debate on drugs too often is presented as a stark either-or proposition—continue to wage "war on drugs" or face up to the reality that this so-called war is unwinnable and consequently, legalize all drugs. This proposition is a false one. While the myriad of flaws that accompany the war on drugs are plain to see for all those willing to open their eyes, the potential consequences of a broad legalization policy also include significant risk.

The argument for the legalization of marijuana makes sense. But to believe that the rationale for the legalization of marijuana easily extends to other illegal drugs ignores the very real differences among them. As Peter Rueter noted in Congressional testimony in 2009, "Cannabis, though more widely used is simply not where the big problems are."[1] In reality, the factors that make legalization of marijuana a reasonable option weigh against the broad legalization of other illegal drugs, particularly cocaine/crack, heroin and methamphetamine. The four of these drugs account for "close to 90% of the social costs associated with the purely illegal drugs."[2]

How is marijuana use different when compared to other illegal drug usage? Most notably, the use of marijuana is prevalent through our society with over 40% of Americans having used marijuana. (1) For Americans aged 20-29, the percent having used marijuana is over 50%.[3] No other illegal drug can claim anywhere even close to that level of acceptance. After marijuana, powder cocaine is the most popular illegal drug. While over 14% of Americans have tried powder cocaine, only 2.5% have used it within the past year and only 1% could be classified as current users (within the previous month).[4] Crack cocaine, while the focus of much of the media coverage of drug problems, is used by only a tiny percentage of Americans. Just over three percent of Americans have tried crack, with less than one percent having used crack within the previous year and less than one-half of one percent using within the past month.[5]

Heroin is used by an even smaller proportion of the population. Less than two percent of Americans have ever used heroin, with only one-tenth of one percent using within the last thirty days. LSD, Ecstasy, and Methamphetamine all show similar patterns. Current users (defined by usage in the prior month) of each of these drugs amount to less than one half of one percent.[6]

Numerically, a larger problem is the nonmedical use of prescription pain relievers, tranquilizers, and sedatives. Diversion of prescription medicine into the illegal market is a significant issue. Diversion ranges from a teenager taking a parent's medication to addicted doctors falsifying prescriptions to feed their own habits. While pharmaceutical diversion does not receive the notoriety that other illegal drug activity engenders, significant criminal justice resources are invested in fighting diversion.

While marijuana use does carry certain risks, the dangers associated with other illegal drug use dwarf those associated with marijuana. First is the risk of addiction. Although the addiction rate for marijuana is relatively low, there are a percentage of marijuana users who will become dependent. While the addictive potential for marijuana use is low, the same cannot be said for other popular illegal drugs. Addiction is a complex phenomenon that involves interplay of the individual and environment as well as the pharmacologic characteristics of the particular drug of choice. While the risks of addiction to a particular drug are difficult to quantify, there is no argument that the risks for addiction associated with cocaine/crack, heroin, and/or methamphetamine are significantly higher than for marijuana. From a policy perspective, it is important to remember that addicted individuals account for not only a disproportionate share of the demand for drugs, but for the majority of the drug related problems afflicting our communities.

Most of the current drug policy discussion focuses on what is seen as a two-sided strategy: demand reduction on the one hand and supply reduction on the other. Supply reduction refers primarily to law enforcement efforts, internationally and locally, to interdict and confiscate drugs before they reach the user. Demand reduction involves implementation of effective prevention programs as well as treatment for addicts to essentially take them out of the drug market. The bulk of the current U.S. policy discussion has been on the ratio of funding provided to supply side strategies versus demand reduction strategies. Over the past several years, federal drug expenditures "averaged 70% for supply reduction and 30% for demand reduction."[7] It is unclear that simply modifying the funding stream within the current supply-demand framework will have much impact as "neither can show much evidence of success."[8]

For drugs other than marijuana, the challenge is to design a policy framework that substantially reduces the demand for drugs and cuts off the flow of billions of dollars to trafficking organizations that directly threaten our national security; minimize the impact of drug use on communities; reduce the health related consequences of drug use, most notably HIV/AIDS and drug overdoses; and accomplish this in an effective, fair and cost efficient manner.

Some of the broad policy goals related to the major illegal drugs, cocaine/crack, heroin and meth, are:

- Significantly reduce the size of the illegal drug market, thus choking off the supply of funds to traffickers.
- Create multiple opportunities to divert users and addicts from the criminal justice system into a health-care/treatment system.
- Focus criminal sanctions on drug related behavior that negatively impacts local neighborhoods and communities.
- Increase harm reduction measures to minimize the impact of drug use on both the individual and the community.

There are a number of specific policy steps that can be implemented in furtherance of these goals. Some of the steps involve change in existing laws and some will require a major shift in how drug use and addiction problems are treated. Each policy recommendation and a short synopsis providing the rationale for the recommendation follow.

For all drug possession instances, replace the criminal offense and process with an administrative violation and process.

This action provides a stronger response than the simple decriminalization of drug possession. The major impact of this change would be minimizing the stigma associated with drug addiction. Experience in other countries clearly supports the notion that stigma is the major barrier to addicts seeking treatment, and there is no reason to believe that addicts in America would react any differently. Through the use of an administrative process similar to the Dissuasion Commission Model in Portugal, the number of addicts entering treatment can be significantly expanded. Police time in arresting and processing drug offenders would be reduced, other costs of the criminal justice response including imprisonment would be reduced and the lifelong consequences to individuals of a criminal conviction would be minimized. Administrative bodies to process, monitor and provide necessary services would need to be developed but could certainly be done at a lower cost than the current criminal justice system.

Each addict coming into treatment represents a high volume buyer in the drug market. In Portugal, in the years following a similar reform, the number of addicts in treatment increased nearly 400%. While the benefits of such a change are far reaching, the most important benefit would be a reduction in the number of buyers in the drug market that in turn, chokes off the money spigot supporting traffickers.

Create a drug treatment system that includes heroin maintenance programs as well as low threshold programs to involve addicts with less motivation for treatment.

Treatment programs for heroin addicts have been less than a resounding success. Reuter notes that, "Long-term follow studies of people in heroin treatment show that after 33 years, the most common way of becoming abstinent is to die."[9]

Methadone programs have been the most widely used method for heroin addiction around the world. However, a recent study from Britain shows that providing heroin to addicts as part of a treatment program may be much more successful.

Addicts were given heroin within a medically supervised setting. The heroin was provided as part of a larger program that included intensive counseling and treatment. The results were striking. "The use of street heroin was reduced by three quarters and the crimes committed trying to get drugs were cut by two-thirds."[10] One of the patients quoted in the study provided an eloquent statement on the role of stigma in her new found success. "The morality of it was taken out of the question. I wasn't being condemned for it and at last I could start taking responsibility in a rational way."[11]

There is not currently good evidence for an analogous form of substitution treatment for cocaine or meth addiction. While the development of a drug that would be an integral part of a substitution treatment regimen for cocaine or meth addiction "remains one of NIDA's top research priorities," current treatment consists of "counseling, social supports and other services."[12]

Keeping in mind that the goal is to increase the number of addicts in treatment, creating a range of programs, including those "low threshold" programs as in the Netherlands, can help meet this goal. Encouraging drug treatment in routine medical practice as opposed to specialized drug treatment programs, an innovation that is also part of the Dutch policy network, could also increase the number of addicts in treatment. There are likely some addicts who shun specialized drug treatment programs who might accept treatment in a general medical setting. Even if the "low threshold" patients have a lower success rate, increasing the overall number of treated addicts will have a positive net effect on the illegal drug market.

To protect citizens and neighborhoods from the effects of drug use and addiction, focus criminal sanctions on drug-related behavior.

There are three specific law changes that can act to isolate and contain drug problems in neighborhoods and public places.

- PROHIBIT PUBLIC USE OF DRUGS. The legalization of marijuana and decriminalization of other drugs *does not* constitute permission to use drugs in public places. Much in the same fashion that local open flask ordinances prohibit public consumption of alcohol and smoking bans prohibit tobacco use in certain public areas, use of drugs in public places should be prohibited and subject to criminal penalties. This would act to minimize some of the problems associated with public use of drugs. Arrests for these violations would also provide an opportunity to move an addict into treatment through use of a Drug Court type program.

- KEEP THE SALE OF DRUGS A CRIMINAL OFFENSE BUT EQUALIZE THE PENALTIES FOR BUYER AND SELLER. As a police officer at every rank, I attended scores of community meetings where drug dealing was the topic. Inevitably, the issue of the "caravan" of suburbanites coming to inner-city neighborhoods to buy drugs was raised. It rarely went unremarked that the sellers, mostly African-American, were likely to be arrested while the buyers, mostly white, did not seem to face similar risks. It is a fairness issue and in the terms of the motherly wisdom imparted to most of us, "It takes two to tango."

    To be effective, the ordinance should set penalties at a relatively low misdemeanor level. It has been my experience that the certainty of a moderate criminal penalty is more a deterrent than a harsh potential penalty which is less likely. As criminal penalties increase, offenders will demand jury trails, attorneys will deploy the significant delaying tactics at their disposal, and prosecutors and judges will be more apt to plea bargain as these cases clog the court dockets.

    As noted above, each arrest should be viewed as an opportunity to move both buyer and seller into treatment, if needed, through a mechanism like Drug Court. Repeat offenses would bring enhanced penalties. Current court handling of DUI offenders offers a good model.

- STRUCTURE IN ENHANCED PENALTIES FOR DRUG SALES IN PUBLIC PLACES. Thousands of drug transactions occur every day that never come to the attention of the authorities nor do they cause any difficulty for anyone outside those directly involved in the transaction. They occur out of the public realm, in homes, apartments, and in hotel rooms. Compare the impact of these transactions with those that accompany the open air drug markets found in every city in the country. Street drug markets have a devastating impact on neighborhoods. These drug sales are accompanied by prostitution, disorderly street behavior and frequent violence. Local businesses struggle as customers shun the location and residents are terrorized and intimidated by the traffickers.

Enhanced criminal penalties for public drug transactions would have the effect of pushing these activities out of the public eye. It would make it more difficult for commuting buyers to locate drug dealers and would move the bulk of the transactions out of the public realm. The shrinking of these drug markets would also lessen the neighborhood deterioration characterized by drug activity.

Perhaps the biggest impact on neighborhood drug markets would be the result of the legalization of marijuana. Moving marijuana sales to legitimate business enterprises would take a huge chunk out of the illegal drug market. This "separation of the markets" provides a barrier between the marijuana purchasers and the street drug dealer that would result in the loss of significant revenue for the traffickers. It would also have a significant impact on the level of street violence. In California, where there is now a "gray market" for marijuana under the state's medical marijuana law, the contrast between the market for this quasi-legal marijuana and the street drug market is dramatic. David Samuels, a reporter with New Yorker Magazine, writes of his experience among the entrepreneurs capitalizing on the sales opportunity under California's medical marijuana law. "The people I met in the high-end ganja business had an affinity for higher modes of thinking and being, including vegetarianism and eating organic food, practicing yoga, avoiding prescription drugs in favor of holistic healing methods, travelling to Indonesia and Thailand, fasting, and experimenting with hallucinogenic drugs. Many were also financially savvy, working long hours and making six-figure incomes."[13] Samuels contrasts that with street drug markets, a "sinister world of urban dope dealers, who flaunt muscles and guns, and charge exorbitant prices for mediocre product."[14] Putting aside Samuels' admiration for yoga-practicing vegans, his comparison of the potential for violence between the marijuana business market and illegal street market is right on point.

Implement Drug Court Programs to handle the offenders who enter the system as a result of their drug related behavior.

As of December of 2007, there were over 2000 Drug Court programs in operation in the United States.[15] Drug Court programs represent a unique blend of the criminal justice system with drug treatment programs in a coordinated and intense effort to intervene with and successfully treat addicts. Studies of drug courts across the country have documented that Drug Court participants have higher rates of treatment success, significant reductions in criminal behavior and substantially better outcomes than drug offenders processed through normal court channels.

Drug Courts are structured in a variety of fashions. Some operate as a diversion type program, with criminal charges dropped if the offender successfully completes the program. Others operate as post conviction programs, with offenders on probation under the supervision of Drug Court personnel. The particular structure of the program does not appear to be a factor in its effectiveness, as both the pre-conviction and post-conviction models show impressive results.[16]

In research studies done in jurisdictions throughout the country, Drug Court outcomes have been positive. Studies in Salt Lake City and Cincinnati are typical. A study in Salt Lake City found that on follow-up, control group participants had three times the re-arrest rate of drug court graduates and almost twice the re-arrest rate of participants in drug court who failed to complete the program. A Cincinnati drug court study found participants less likely to be arrested and less likely to have multiple re-arrests than a comparison group.[17] Studies in Portland, OR, Suffolk, MA, and a statewide evaluation on drug courts in California have all found similar results. The positive results have occurred regardless of the drug of choice of the offender.[18] The programs have also documented success even for long-term addicts, including those viewed as high risk or incorrigible.[19]

Drug courts appear to be cost effective. A study in California found the cost/client in drug court averaging about $3000 but concluded the drug court intervention saved $11,000 in long term costs.[20] Similar studies in other jurisdictions have also found significant cost benefits associated with Drug Court programs.[21]

As drug courts appear to be successful with even the most difficult addicts, and regardless of the particular structure of the program, it is worth noting that the key ingredient in drug court success is creating an atmosphere of concern for the addict, combined with good treatment services and a "tough love" approach by court officials. First person accounts by drug court graduates are nearly universal in their recognition of the compassion and caring shown throughout the drug court experience as a key factor in their recovery. One graduate eloquently captures the role of caring by drug court staff in her own recovery:

> They don't do it for the glamour and prestige that comes from working with a bunch of addicts. They do it because they truly care. To them, we are not bad people trying to get good, but, rather, sick people trying to get well. We lie to them, we fight them, and, I am willing to bet, we sometimes even break their hearts, and yet, they are still there... They know, in our pasts, we have almost destroyed the lives of those who love us more than anything in the world, and done things so horrific we can hardly bear to speak of them, and, the damndest thing is, they are *still* there. Well, I am here today as a testament to what becomes of a person when drug court is always "there." And as long as I live, I will be grateful to drug court for being there.[22]

Implement needle exchange programs, drug testing, overdose education, and other harm reduction measures to minimize the impact of drug use on both the individual and the community.

It is beyond dispute that harm reductions measures can effectively reduce the HIV/AIDS rate among IV drug users as well as prevent overdose deaths. Congressional debate in 2009 on federal funding for needle exchange programs confirms that these efforts remain controversial with limited public support. The lack of community support that prevents public funding for harm reduction measures does not mean these measures cannot be implemented. In nearly every community, there will be a group of individuals with the resources and skills to provide these programs without government funding. As the stigma surrounding drug addiction begins to wane, there will be increasing public support of harm reduction programs.

Create a national network of evidence-based primary prevention programs and strengthen the ability of both governmental and private organizations to intervene effectively at an early stage in the addiction process.

As with almost every other health problem, primary prevention is the most cost effective approach. Long term research on effective primary prevention programs has identified a number of key elements underpinning the success of these programs.[23] Lack of funding and competing educational priorities have been the biggest barriers to a more widespread implementation of these programs. Yet an investment in these programs may pay off in markedly reduced future treatment and social costs. The National Institute on Drug Abuse estimates that for every dollar invested in primary prevention, a future savings of $10 in treatment costs alone can be recouped.[24] A portion of the tax revenues generated through marijuana legalization should be earmarked to support those prevention programs with a proven track record of success.

Along with increased primary prevention efforts, early intervention programs should be widely implemented. Intervention with drug users is now a well established feature of American culture and is even the subject of a popular television series, *Intervention*, broadcast on the A&E network. On the show, now on the air over ten years, addicts are confronted by family members and friends and urged to enter drug treatment. Over the life of the series, *Intervention* has shown 125 actual interventions and the network says 102 of the individuals featured on the show remain drug free.[25]

Most government and many private organizations currently have in place programs designed to intervene with employees struggling with drug problems. These programs, generally referred to as EAPs or Employee Assistance Programs, have an established track record of success and an expansion of these programs would bring significant numbers of addicts into treatment.

DISCUSSION

The steps outlined above would have a major impact on the overall illegal drug market, as well as its street corner distribution network. The legalization of marijuana would remove a significant piece of the drug market. Of the total population of current (within the previous 30 days) illegal drug consumers, 42.6% were marijuana only consumers.[26] Thus, the legalization of marijuana, in and of itself, would remove over 40% of the buyers from the illegal market. Marijuana proceeds are an estimated 60% of the total revenue supporting Mexican drug traffickers.[27] The business of drug trafficking is similar to other enterprises and not many businesses could financially withstand the loss of 60% of their revenue.

Without marijuana as the anchor for their illegal drug menu, traffickers would be left with a pool of buyers that includes three groups. The largest group consists of addicts, those who are heavy users and are involved in seeking and using drugs as a primary activity. Some addicts who have been in treatment will relapse and re-enter the market. Addicts in prison may re-join the market following their release.

Murder of a Police Detective

The severed head of Detective Rolondo Flores was delivered to a Mexican Army Base a few days after Flores was assigned the investigation into the 2011 shooting of David Hartley, an American tourist shot while jet-skiing on Falcon Lake, a tourist destination on the U.S. Mexican border. Mexican officials later named members of the Zeta drug cartel as suspects in the shooting but no arrests have been made in either murder.[28]

A second group is casual users, who are not currently addicted but will purchase drugs on an infrequent and irregular basis. Some percentage of casual users will become addicted and morph into heavy consumers.

The third group is the new customers who are needed by the market to replace those who enter treatment, are jailed, or die. Dealers have been creative in seeking new customers, providing free samples, discounts, and a variety of products to entice new users. Police investigating a meth lab in Arkansas in 2006 were shocked to find packets of "Strawberry Quick" drink mix being used in the meth formula. The sugary mix gives the drug a pink coloring, making it less threatening for new users. The sugary children's drink has been found in meth labs in Missouri, Wisconsin, Texas and Washington State. Steve Robertson, a DEA spokesman noted, "Traffickers are out there and are trying to sell it to customers, whether they are young customers or older, brand-new customers by changing the color or the taste or just giving it a less-intimidating name, they are trying to make it seem less dangerous and lure this new customer base."[29]

Our challenge is to remove as many of those addicted customers as possible out of the market, discourage casual users from even infrequent use of the market, minimize the number of new customers coming into the market, and shorten the addiction (drug buying) careers of those who do enter the market. The challenge is to accomplish these goals in a significant enough manner to threaten the economic underpinnings that support the illegal drug enterprise.

The potential impact of the recommended policy changes on the illegal market are significant, particularly those steps that will increase the number of addicts in treatment. As previously noted, those consumers seeking the four major categories of drugs (cocaine, crack, heroin, and methamphetamine) account for 90% of our related social problems.[30] The majority of these drug buyers are addicted. They account for a disproportionate share of the demand for these drugs. Thus, each addict (high volume buyer) entering treatment represents more of a loss to the market than a casual buyer. NIDA estimates that currently, only 10.8% of American drug addicts get treatment.[31] It is difficult to guess exactly what level of increase might be expected, but the Portuguese experience supports the potential of a large increase. From 1999 to 2003, the number of addicts in Portuguese treatment increased by 147%[32] and by 2008, in just under 10 years, the number of addicts in treatment nearly quadrupled.[33] If the drug market loses 20% to 30% or, at the top end, 40% of its high volume customers, it would likely mean a loss in total revenue that substantially exceeds those percentages.

Another place where the illegal market could be significantly impacted is within the nation's local, state, and federal prison systems. The drug abuse rates of the nation's criminal offenders are estimated at more than 400% higher than the general population. A Bureau of Justice study found that 53% of state prisoners and 45 % of federal prisoners were drug dependent.[34] As these inmates are released back to the community without any treatment for their drug problem, they are likely to reenter the drug market. Treatment will be effective for a significant percentage of these people. Per NIDA studies, "treating addicts in prison reduces their later drug use by 50-70 percent and their later criminality and resulting arrests by 50-60 percent."[35] Each prisoner who returns to the community drug free also represents the loss of a high volume customer in the drug market.

Directly taking customers out of the market by moving them into treatment would be the most significant step in reducing drug trafficking, but it is not the only possibility. The number of casual buyers in the market can also be reduced. These buyers, by definition, are less committed to the market than addicts and thus can be more easily deterred. Some will be scared out of the market by the increased risk of arrest and the criminal penalties represented by an enforcement focus on buyers as well as sellers. Forcing the market out of the public realm will also make it more difficult for the casual buyer to find drugs and the less motivated of these buyers will simply choose not to participate.

Slowing the initiation of new users into the market is a significant challenge. Without a supply of new customers to replace those larger numbers going into treatment, the illegal drug market will begin to wither. Expanding primary prevention programs can remove a segment of the population at risk. Accomplishing a "separation of the markets" through marijuana legalization will also cripple the movement of new users into the market. Most new users of the drug market are introduced through the purchase of marijuana and breaking that connection limits new users' access to the market.

For those new users who do become addicted, the challenge is to shorten their addiction careers. Early intervention through families, employers and the criminal justice system will cut short their active addiction period. Lessening the stigma associated with drug addiction will create a social environment making it easier to move addicted individuals into the treatment system.

These changes will come easily or quickly. As the debate on marijuana legalization quickens, a poor economy and the appetite of government of all levels for new tax revenue will drive the effort forward. Defenders of the current prohibition approach are dwindling and pressure for change continues to build. Gil Kerlikowske, the current federal Drug Czar, in a nicely understated tone, notes "not many people think the drug war is a success."[36]

Recognizing the obvious and beginning a national discussion on rational alternatives will be the beginning of a new approach to the country's drug problem.

*Figures on drug use are from the National Household Drug Use Survey. The entire report is available at http://www.oas.samhsa.gov/

NOTES

1. Rueter, Peter and Caulkins, Jonathan. (2009) "An Assessment of Drug Incarceration and Foreign Interventions." Testimony before the House Oversight and Government Reform Committee, May 19, 2009.
2. Ibid.
3. NSDUH (2009). National Survey on Drug Use and Health. http://www.oas.samhsa.gov/. Retrieved October 22, 2009. Table 1.12B.
4. Ibid, Table 1.29B.
5. Ibid, Table 1.22B.
6. Ibid.
7. Duncan, D.F., & Nicholson, T. (1997). "Dutch drug policy; A model for America?" Journal of Health and Social Policy, 8(3), 1-15.
8. Ibid, p.1.
9. Rueter and Caulkins (2009). "An Assessment of Drug Incarceration and Foreign Interventions."
10. Newton, Paula. (2009) "Study Touts Treating Heroin Addicts with Heroin." *CNN News*, October 20, 2009. http://www.cnn.com/2009/HEALTH/10/20/treating.with.heroin/index.html#cnnSTCText. Retrieved October 29, 2009.
11. Ibid.
12. NIDA (2009). *NIDA Info Facts: Crack and Cocaine*. National Institute of Drug Abuse, Washington, D.C., June, 2009. http://www.nida.nih.gov/infofacts/. Retrieved October 12, 2009.
13. Samuels, David. (2009). "How Medical Marijuana is Transforming the Pot Industry." *New Yorker Magazine*. July 28, 2009.
14. Ibid.

15. Huddleston, C.West, Marlowe, Douglas, Casebolt, Rachel. (2008) "Painting the Current Picture: A National Report Card on Drug Courts and Other Problem-Solving Court Programs in the United States." Bureau of Justice Assistance, Department of Justice, May 2008.

16. Ibid.

17. Johnson, Shelley and Latessa, Edward. (2000) "The Hamilton County Drug Court: Outcome Evaluation Findings." Center for Criminal Justice Research, University of Cincinnati. July, 2000.

18. Huddleston, Marlowe & Casebolt. (2008). "Painting the Current Picture: A National Report Card on Drug Courts and Other Problem-Solving Court Programs in the United States." Bureau of Justice Assistance, Department of Justice, May 2008.

19. Marlowe, D.B. (2006). "Judicial Supervision of Drug-Abusing Offenders." *Journal of Psychoactive Drugs, SARC Supplement* 3, 323-331.

20. Carey, S. M., Finigan, M., Crumpton. D., & Waller, M. (2006). "California Drug Courts: Outcomes, Costs and Promising Practices." An overview of phase II in a statewide study. *Journal of Psychoactive Drugs, SARC Supplement* 3, 345-356.

21. Huddleston, Marlowe & Casebolt. (2008). "Painting the Current Picture."

22. Ibid, 15.

23. NIDA (2004). *NIDA Info Facts: Lessons from Prevention Research*. National Institute of Drug Abuse, Washington, D.C., June, 2009. http://www.nida.nih.gov/infofacts/. Retrieved October 20, 2009.

24. Ibid.

25. A&E (2009). "A&E Network's Award-Winning Series "Intervention" Returns For A Seventh Season Monday, May 25 At 9pm Et/Pt." Released by A&E May 5, 2009.

26. NSDUH (2009). Table G5.

27. Fainaru, Steve and Booth, William. (2009) "Cartels Face an Economic Battle." *Washington Post*, October 7, 2009. http://www.washingtonpost.com/wp-dyn/content/article/2009/10/06/AR2009100603847.html. Retrieved 10/30/2009.

28. *CBS News* – Crimesider. David Hartley Update. http://www.cbsnews.com/8301-504083_162-20020054-504083.html. Downloaded 6/15/2011.

29. Gambrell, Jon (2009, February11). "Candy-Flavored Meth Targets New Users." Associated Press. Retrieved from http://www.cbsnews.com/stories/2007/05/02/health/main2752266.shtml.

30. Rueter and Caulkins (2009). "An Assessment of Drug Incarceration and Foreign Interventions."

31. NIDA (2008). NIDA Info Facts: Treatment Statistics. National Institute of Drug Abuse, Washington, D.C., June, 2008. http://www.nida.nih.gov/infofacts. Retrieved June 15, 2009.

32. Greenwald, Glenn (2009). *Drug Decriminalization in Portugal: Lessons for Creating Fair and Successful Drug Policies*. CATO Institute, Washington, D.C.

33. *Economist*, (2009). "Portugal's Drug Policy: Treating, not Punishing." Lisbon, August 27, 2009.

34. Fletcher, Bennett and Chandler, Redonna (2009). "Principles of Drug Abuse Treatment for Criminal Justice Populations." National Institute of Drug Abuse. http://www.nida.nih.gov. Retrieved October 29, 2009.

35. Lershner, Alan. (2005). "Why Should We Treat Addicts Anyway? The Solution We Refuse to Use." National Institute on Drug Abuse (NIDA), Director's page. http://www.nida.nih.gov/. Retrieved 10/24/2009.

36. Will, George. (2009). "Maybe We Can Learn Yet To Say No To Drugs." *Cincinnati Enquirer*, p. A15, October 29, 2009.

Chapter 10

The Costs of Policy Paralysis

> *Oakland has become the first city in the country to authorize large-scale industrial pot cultivation . . . Opponents argue the urban pot farms will put small growers out of business.*
>
> USA Today
> July 28, 2010

In an ideal world, law makers would act with deliberation in developing policy to meet carefully crafted goals. Yet much of our drug policy discussion has resembled what one writer described as "the country's 40-year-old on-again, off-again shouting match."[1] Today, the cutting edge of the drug policy debate is centered on marijuana and the steady policy slide away from prohibition. While our policy recommendation of full legalization remains a distant goal, a description of some necessary steps to legalization is instructive.

It is again worth noting that despite much of the public conversation about legalizing marijuana, the fact remains that no other country in the world has taken the legalization step. Many countries have decriminalized possession of marijuana and some countries have replaced criminal penalties with administrative sanctions. Yet no country has yet taken the step of moving marijuana from its illegal status into a legally controlled and regulated market. In view of its strong prohibitionist history, for the American federal government to take this step would be a radical and, at least for the immediate future, an unlikely move.

At least part of the reluctance to take this step is the United Nations Single Convention on Narcotic Drugs, of which the United States has been an active advocate. This international treaty, first signed in 1961, commits those nations that are signatories, to criminalize the cultivation, manufacture, offering for sale and possession of a long laundry list of drugs including cannabis. This treaty has been updated over the years and 180 nations are now a party to the Single Convention.[2]

Even if it were so inclined, for the United States to pull back or abrogate from an international treaty would have serious repercussions far beyond drug policy and that is unlikely to occur. Modification of the treaty would appear to be an alternative but experts note that under UN rules, modification would be very difficult.[3] For the United States to legalize marijuana and still honor the UN treaty would likely require a constitutional amendment. Fazey notes that:

> Many articles in the conventions are prefaced by the words "subject to its constitutional principles and the basic concepts of its legal system." This has been used by the USA not to implement part of article 3 of the 1988 Convention, which prevents inciting others to use narcotic or psychotropic drugs, on the basis that this would be in contravention of their constitutional amendment guaranteeing freedom of speech.[4]

Any constitutional change that would allow legalization of cannabis would be a long and laborious process although it is worth noting that both national alcohol prohibition and its repeal were accomplished via the constitutional amendment process. What seems more likely is that the movement toward marijuana legalization will be led by state and local jurisdictions.

Today, state authorities, sometimes driven by ballot initiatives, are moving marijuana policy in the direction of legalization. Particularly on the medical marijuana issue, the federal government in 2009 has been forced into a catch-up role, notifying officials in the 14 states that had approved medical marijuana at that time that federal authorities will not prosecute those citizens complying with state law.

Meanwhile, citizens across the country, from voter referendums to actions by local legislators, have signaled a growing impatience with current drug policy. An additional 15 states are considering medical marijuana ballot initiatives and on Election Day, 2009, voters in Breckenridge, Colorado approved the legalization of marijuana in their town. The legalization was approved by a vote of 73 percent to 27 percent.[5]

The current policy drift as much as the country moves to a de facto legalization provides an object lesson on both of the pitfalls of a policy vacuum as well as the potential benefit of marijuana legalization. The medical marijuana market in California and, to a lesser extent, in other states, is providing an important example.

Medical marijuana was first approved in California in 1996. There are currently an estimated 400,000 patients approved for medical marijuana and these patients receive their marijuana through about 700 state sanctioned dispensaries.[6] Legislation attempting to clarify the regulations controlling the medical marijuana market was passed in 2003 and included a provision allowing California counties to set their own regulations. The result has been a "patchwork of rules and regulations" that allows growers in some counties to cultivate up to 99 plants for a qualified patient.[7] The confusing and contradictory policy network has contributed to a dramatic escalation of the domestic marijuana market, which increased an estimated 1000% in recent years.[8]

The medical conditions approved for prescribed marijuana have also expanded. Originally proposed primarily as an aid for cancer patients, Californians now are prescribed marijuana for serious conditions like AIDS, glaucoma, epilepsy and multiple sclerosis as well as relief for general symptoms such as nausea, loss of appetite, menstrual pain, sleeplessness, and mild anxiety.

Growers for the medical marijuana market have sought to separate their products from the competition, developing products with a variety of odors, texture and taste. One marijuana chain store, the Farmacy, "employs a pastry chef to oversee production of all its baked goods."[9] Competition in the medical market has also led to marketing battles over branding and a variety of marijuana based products. Popular brands include L.A. Confidential, Purple Kush, Lavender, Sour Diesel, Jedi, Bubba Kush and AK Mist. Marijuana-laced products available include brownies, granola, honeys, cookies, butters, cooking oils, chocolate wafers and lollipops. Marijuana is available for smoking or in "capsules, lozenges, spray-under-the-tongue tinctures, and even topically applied salves."[10]

One California pot entrepreneur has developed a vending machine to provide convenience for his medical marijuana patients. The machine would dispense an ounce of marijuana to pre-approved patients who would access the product via a special prepaid card and a fingerprint identification reader attached to the machine. Patients could choose from Platinum Kush, Fire O.G., Bubba Kush, Purple Kush and Wild Cherry.[11]

California is not the only state moving in the direction of legalization. Colorado now has 15 dispensaries operating and in Oregon "nearly one in four active physicians has authorized at least one of his patients to grow marijuana for medical use."[12] One state that is taking the business of medical marijuana very seriously is New Mexico, which is taking steps to establish state-sanctioned marijuana farms to supply its marijuana patients. The state is licensing nonprofits to grow marijuana and has a waiting list of agencies awaiting state approval.[13]

While the lack of a coherent regulatory system has spawned an unregulated market with no controls on potency or ingredients, the growth of the domestic marijuana industry has illustrated the potential for a legitimate market to put the illegal traffickers out of business. Law enforcement and American marijuana growers agree that "stiff competition from thousands of mom-and-pop marijuana farmers in the United States threatens the bottom line for powerful Mexican drug organizations in a way that decades of arrests and seizures have not."[14]

With the federal government unwilling or unable to act, the development of a regulatory system for legal marijuana would fall to the states, much in the same fashion as states did at the end of alcohol prohibition. States are now beginning to develop controls over the medical marijuana market. The federal government could facilitate this process with a declaration, similar their 2009 statement on medical marijuana, that the federal government will not arrest citizens who are in compliance with state marijuana legalization laws.

Individual states would then be free to legalize marijuana within their own jurisdiction or not. If they chose to make marijuana a legal product, a regulatory system would need to be implemented. States could approve certain marijuana products, implement a state inspection and certification process and license marijuana distributors at both the wholesale and retail levels. Some states, much in the fashion of the current state alcohol rules, might choose to implement a state monopoly on marijuana production and sale. A variety of other regulation would come into play, including product potency, ingredients, distribution network, hours of sale, age limitations, and a plethora of others.

It would be reasonable to implement some cooperative agreements among states on potency limits, legal movement of marijuana back and forth across state lines and others. It is worth noting that although the process appears daunting, it is a process our country has previously gone through at the end of alcohol prohibition.

> **Drug Complaint Leads to Murder**
>
> Angela Dawson stood up to the drug dealers in her Baltimore neighborhood and paid with her life. Dawson and her husband grew tired of the drug traffic in front of their house and in the fall of 2002, called the police 35 times complaining about the dealers. The dealers threw Molotov cocktails into the Dawson's home, forcing the couple and their five children into the street. Despite an offer from authorities to place them in the witness protection program, the Dawsons declared they would not be run out of their own neighborhood by drug thugs. On October 16, 2002, Darrel Brooks, a 21 year-old dealer who'd repeatedly clashed with the Dawsons, kicked in their front door and splashed a jar of gasoline around the living room and then ignited it. Angela and Carnell Dawson, along with their five children, were killed in the fire.[15]

Tax policy would certainly be an issue as the potential amount of money in a legal marijuana market is significant. Taxes and fees at every stage, from the state approved growers of legal marijuana to the wholesalers to the retail distribution network, could provide a needed infusion of support for state and local governments. Some earmarking of funds for drug treatment and prevention services would be a reasonable option.

DISCUSSION

Action by voters and legislators across the country is demonstrating that Americans want to end marijuana prohibition. Policy-makers, particularly at the

Federal level, are in the uncomfortable position of clinging to a prohibitionist posture in the face of the reality of changing community sentiment. The choices are stark. If leaders at both the Federal and state level ignore drug policy reform, voter-led initiatives and local communities such as Breckenridge will leave them behind. The result will be an escalation of a marijuana market with minimal concern for product and consumer safety and operating with little or no governmental oversight. This lack of government oversight will be compounded by the failure to impose the regulation and taxes under which other business enterprises must operate.

More importantly, the government will have lost the opportunity to strike at the terror grip of drug cartels, particularly on the Mexican border. It is difficult to overstate the gravity of that situation. With proceeds largely derived from the marijuana business, drug cartels are directly threatening the Mexican government. The drug-related murder rate doubled in 2008 and in February of 2009, Mexican General Angeles Dahuajare announced that "more than 17,000 soldiers had deserted in 2008."[16] Many of the deserters join drug gangs who offer the soldiers better pay.

A 2009 operation by the Army's Asymmetrical Warfare Group (AWG) found drug cartels teaming with terrorists along the 2000 mile Mexican border. The conclusions of the AWG report are blunt and disturbing:

> Drug-related assassinations and kidnappings [in Mexico] are now commonplace occurrences throughout the country. Squad-sized units of the police and army have been tortured, murdered, and their decapitated bodies left on public display. The malignancy of drug criminality now contaminates not only the 2000 miles of cross-border U.S. communities, but stretches throughout the United States in more than 295 cities.[17]

The blossoming of the medical marijuana market in California has demonstrated the potential to take the funding out from under the cartels. Marijuana proceeds account for an estimated 60% of the cartels' revenue.[18] Starving them of this funding will cripple their ability to continue terror activity on both sides of the border.

NOTES

1. Parloff, Roger. (2009). "How Marijuana Became Legal." *Fortune Magazine*. September 18, 2009. On-line edition. http://rss.cnn.com/rss/magazines_fortune.rss. Retrieved November 2, 2009.
2. Single Convention on Narcotic Drugs (2009) Wikipedia. http://en.wikipedia.org/wiki/Single_Convention_on_Narcotic_Drugs#Influence_on_domestic_legislation. Retrieved 11/3/2009.
3. Fazey, Cindy. (2003) "The UN Drug Policies and the Prospect for Change." http://www.fuoriluogo.it/arretrati/2003/apr_17_en.htm. Retrieved November 3 2009.
4. Ibid.

5. Gathright, Alan (2009, November 3). "Breckenridge Pot Legalization Creates Big Buzz." TheDenverChannel.com, http://www.thedenverchannel.com/news/21515178/detail.html, Retrieved September 9, 2011.
6. Parloff, "How Marijuana Became Legal."
7. Samuels, David (2008, July 28). "How medical marijuana is transforming the pot industry." *The New Yorker*, http://www.newyorker.com/reporting/2008/07/28/080728fa_fact_samuels, Retrieved September 9, 2011.
8. Ibid.
9. Parloff, "How Marijuana Became Legal."
10. Ibid.
11. Lowery, Brandon. "Marijuana Machines Could Be Cure For Inconvenience." L.A. Daily News, on-line edition, 1/29/2009. http://labs.daylife.com/journalist/brandon_lowrey. Retrieved November 2, 2009.
12. Parloff, "How Marijuana Became Legal."
13. Jojola, Jeremy and Kappus, Matthew. "Medical Marijuana Grower to Begin Distribution." *KOB.com*, posted 6/3/2009. http://www.kob.com/article/stories/S961683.shtml. Retrieved November 2, 2009.
14. Fainaru, Steve and Booth, William. (2009) "Cartels Face an Economic Battle." *Washington Post*, October 7, 2009. http://www.washingtonpost.com/wp-dyn/content/article/2009/10/06/AR2009100603847.html. Retrieved 10/30/2009.
15. Gettleman, Jeffery. "In Baltimore, Slogan Collides with Reality." *NY Times*, September 2, 2003.
16. Sanchez, Matt. (2009) "Mexican Drug Cartels Armed To the Hilt, Threatening National Security." *Fox News.com*, February 4, 2009. http://www.foxnews.com/story/0,2933,487911,00.html. Retrieved November 4, 2009.
17. Helms, Nat. (2009) "Army Report: Drug Cartels, Terrorists Infiltrate U.S." *Newsmax.com*, June 5, 2009. http://www.newsmax.com/newsfront/mexico_border_fence/2009/06/05/222148.html?utm_medium=RSS. Retrieved November 4, 2009.
18. Fainaru and Booth. (2009).

Chapter 11

A New Direction

> *"And I cannot help but wonder how many more lives, and how much more money, will be wasted before another Robert McNamara admits what is plain for all to see: the war on drugs is a failure."*
>
> Walter Cronkite
> March 1, 2006

Most Americans would agree that drug abuse is a significant problem. But consensus that a problem exists and agreement on solutions are two radically different challenges. At the federal level, on an issue clouded by strong feelings and in a political atmosphere characterized by bickering and partisanship, movement beyond the status quo appears unlikely.

If action by the federal government were the prelude for drug law reform, I would indeed be pessimistic. However, in this era of partisan gridlock in Washington, change will come boiling up from the local and state level. The medical marijuana issue stands as exhibit A that local and state leadership will lead the change with the federal government dragged along. The step from approval of medical marijuana to marijuana as a legal product controlled and regulated in the legitimate market is inevitable. Legalization approval by voters in Breckenridge, Colorado and proposed legislation in California (Proposition 19) in 2010 represent the first trickles of what will eventually could become a torrent of marijuana-related legislative action. Predicting with much precision exactly what may occur would require a time machine but some reasonable guesses can be ventured.

In the next few years, one or more states will legislatively approve marijuana as a legal commodity. While California Proposition 19 proposing marijuana legalization was voted down in November of 2010, that loss may have been due more to the particular details of the referendum than voter sentiment on marijuana legalization. One poll, completed just a few months prior to the election, showed 56% of Californians supporting marijuana legalization.[1] If legalization eventually passes, in California or another state, it will likely be accompanied by the silent acquiescence of the federal government, which will either ignore the development or take a stance similar to their current position on state medical marijuana laws. In other words, the federal government will not take enforcement action against anyone in compliance with state law.

The motivation behind proposed legalization in California was as much about miserable state finances as it was about drug law reform. Those states in the worst financial shape and desperate for new revenue will likely lead the way toward legalization. Under the California proposal, local governments would have been granted the authority to tax marijuana sales, a business estimated at $14 billion annually.[2]

Legalization in any state will include two major thrusts—a heavily regulated business model and a plan for distribution of the revenue to be generated. The legislation will look similar to the various state laws around the country that control legalized gambling. A state commission with wide regulatory authority will be appointed. People serving on the commission will be intensely vetted and anyone with the slightest connection to organized crime or drug trafficking will be not be eligible. The commission will develop an encyclopedic set of regulations controlling the marijuana product to be sold, age restrictions, limitations on retail outlets, advertising, packaging, and the imposition of multiple state revenue collection points from the farm producing the marijuana to sales taxes at the consumer end. Again, similar to state gambling legislation and to gain public support, revenue generated will be earmarked for worthy causes—education, addictions treatment, services for the elderly and so on.

Also, as with legalized gambling, the major concern raised will be the involvement of drug cartels and organized crime. Some police officers of my acquaintance believe that if drugs were to be legalized, the criminal organizations now controlling the illegal market would move seamlessly into the legal market. James Mills, an author who has written extensively on drug cartels, has a trafficker in his novel, *The Hearing*, musing about drug legalization in the United States:

> He [Vicaro] also wanted the decriminalization of marijuana, and eventually, cocaine. He already controlled cocoa plantations, processing labs, and distribution networks. Legalization would

eliminate all the people Vicaro had to pay so liberally to do his illegal processing, shipping, warehousing and retailing. Hundreds of millions of dollars in bribes to Latin American officials would no longer be necessary. Decriminalization would let Vicaro turn his expensively illegal operation into an even more profitable legal enterprise. Another R. J. Reynolds.[3]

The history of legalized gambling along with the ruthless edge of the free market weighs against Vicaro's fantasy. Putting aside the fact that legalization of cocaine is extremely unlikely, the medical marijuana experience in California shows that entrepreneurs in a free market, even the grey market of medical marijuana, will quickly overcome a Vicaro-type business model characterized by violence, bribery and intimidation. The monopoly that real-life Vicaros maintain will crumble when their business is forced to compete in an open marketplace.

Similar fears characterized the transition of gambling from an organized crime controlled activity to a legitimate state regulated business. The fears have not materialized. Legalized gambling enterprises, notably casinos, are operated by publically held and highly respected business organizations including corporate nameplates like Sheratons and Hiltons. They are accountable to shareholders and operate under the scrutiny of the Securities Exchange Commission. Where organized crime has been associated with legalized gambling, it is usually attributable to poor government regulation.[4] As marijuana legalization makes a similar transition, tight regulation and strict government oversight are warranted and will be the best defense against any encroachment by organized crime.

Policy changes directed at the illegal market will suppress the violence that infects these markets. The violence is suffered by both buyers and sellers. For those seeking drugs, it is difficult to overstate the risks inherent in buying illegal drugs on the street. The brief interaction between the drug seller and drug buyer can easily deteriorate from a quick exchange of drugs for money to a serious assault, robbery, rape or homicide. Every day across the country, homicides labeled "drug-related" obscure the tragedy of unwitting buyers getting in over their heads in attempting to buy drugs from individuals who view them much as wolves view sheep.

Violence against buyers constitutes only part of the overall violence picture. Violence among dealers over product, money, and turf account for a large portion of the street violence afflicting our cities. The phenomena of home invasion robberies illustrates the deadly intersection of drug trafficking and violence.

As dealers, particularly at the wholesale level, come into possession of a quantity of drugs, their risk of being ripped off escalates. Word spreads on the street that a particular individual or address has just taken a delivery and rival dealers or gang members may seize the opportunity to mount a home invasion on the location taking both the drugs and the money. In my experience, home invasion robberies are invariably tied to the illegal drug market and our drug unit routinely responded to reports of home invasions. In many of these instances, there was often enough drug evidence left behind to establish charges against the victim of the robbery. One gang operating in Cincinnati in the early 2000's supported their operations by selling quantities of drugs to street dealers, then a short time later, often even the same day, mounting home invasion operations to take the drugs back, repeating the process over and over. In a number of cities, gangs have disguised their home invasion robberies as a police operation, wearing SWAT type clothing and identifying themselves as police officers. This has the effect of making genuine police operations more dangerous as well as undercutting community confidence in the police. These drug rip off schemes create a spiral of violence as victims violently retaliate against those suspected of ripping them off. The failure by a victim to retaliate in full measure marks them as easy prey who will be repeatedly targeted.

In addition to choking off funds to major drug organizations, drug policy change will suppress the violence that characterizes street corner drug markets. The step of moving marijuana to the legitimate market robs the street dealer of the bulk of his customers. By cutting the volume of interaction between buyers and sellers, the level of violence will be dramatically reduced. Changes in the drug market will provide the opportunity to redeploy police resources for safer communities. As the police are the entry point for the criminal justice system, these changes will reverberate through the entire justice system.

CHANGES IN THE CRIMINAL JUSTICE SYSTEM

The policy steps suggested herein have the potential to dramatically change the nature of the work of first-line beat cops. Simply by decriminalizing possession offenses, police officers will be spared hours of wasted time processing minor offenders who pose little or no threat to public safety. Making an arrest in most jurisdictions involves not only significant administrative paperwork but time spent in prisoner transport, evidence processing, and booking the offender into the local jail. This loss is time that could otherwise be spent in addressing crucial community safety priorities. In 2008, over 1.7 million drug arrests were recorded nationally.[5] Drug arrests are the single biggest category of arrests tracked by the FBI and represent over 12% of all arrests made in the country. Marijuana arrests account for about half of the nation's drug arrests and of those, nearly 90% were possession only charges. Over recent years, more police time, as measured by the number of arrests, has been spent on marijuana offenses. Arrests for marijuana reached a record high in 2006[6] translating into more officers tied up in administrative tasks related to arrests with questionable impact on neighborhood safety.

Reduced officer time processing marijuana offenders and a shrinkage in the street dealing as marijuana moves to the legitimate market represents a potential significant increase in police capacity. Some of this capacity can be directed toward investigation of heroin/cocaine/meth trafficking, the drugs which represent the bulk of the social problems. Following similar drug reform in Portugal, police there increased major seizures of drugs by targeting high level dealers. Increased police capacity could also be devoted toward fully implementing the promise of Community Oriented Policing, an effort now hampered at times by inadequate police resources.

Changes in policing will in turn lead to change in the rest of the criminal justice system. Removing marijuana possession offenses means fewer cases on court dockets, smaller caseloads for prosecutors, and probation officers with more time to supervise serious offenders. Some of this new capacity could be directed at the drug addicts who flood the system. Drug courts have clearly proven their worth, and an expansion to accommodate additional drug offenders would be a worthwhile investment.

The recommended movement of drug possession offenses from a criminal process to an administrative violation process represents a major opportunity for positive impact on the justice system. There are a variety of ways in which these administrative boards could be organized and implemented. The Portuguese model of the Dissuasion Commission is a good starting point. The overall goal of this new body is to identify addicts and move them into treatment. By moving this process out of the criminal justice context, the stigma that blocks many addicts from seeking treatment is minimized. Higher numbers of addicts in other countries have sought treatment following this type change and there is no reason to believe American addicts would respond any differently. Staffing for these administrative bodies including personnel to facilitate entry into treatment and monitor treatment outcomes would be needed. This could be accomplished at a lower per capita cost than similar involvement in the criminal justice system. Aspects of the current Drug Court model would become part of the operation.

Even though drug possession will no longer be a criminal offense, addicts will continue to appear in large numbers in the criminal justice system. They will be there on drug related charges including purchase and sale of drugs, driving under the influence, disorderly behavior under the influence and a variety of others. Every addict under court supervision represents an opportunity to take a customer from the illegal market and Drug Court programs, as noted earlier, have a track record of success that is beyond dispute.

CHANGES IN THE DRUG TREATMENT SYSTEM

Successfully choking off the funds supporting the illegal drug market rests primarily on our ability to transition addicts into treatment. Doubling, tripling or even more the number of addicts in treatment is the surest way to reduce the money supporting the drug cartels. Creating treatment capacity for these increased numbers will require a significant expansion of the current drug treatment network. Lowering the stigma associated with drug treatment will increase the number of addicts seeking assistance and effective supervision by both the administrative and criminal systems will create increased demand on community treatment resources.

As the treatment system expands, diversity of treatment options must be a priority. Particular emphasis on low threshold treatment options will be required. The over-arching consideration has to be the recognition that treatment is directly in competition with the illegal drug market for the hearts and dollars of addicts. Recognizing that every addict represents a high volume contributor to the illegal market, the treatment system should make every reasonable effort to recruit and retain addicts in their programs. Not every treatment program needs to take this stance but within the larger treatment system, there must be programs with the ability to engage even the most resistant addicts into treatment. Every day an addict is kept out of the drug market should be viewed as a strike against traffickers. Those that relapse should be as quickly as possible brought back into the system and program success should be judged on the basis of recovery criteria as well as patient retention.

Heroin is one of the quartet of drugs that underlies major social problems. Methadone has historically been a widely used treatment but newer drugs, like Buprenorphine, appear to be a significant improvement over methadone. The use of Buprenorphine provides another treatment option that may entice addicts into treatment. Most importantly, the National Institute on Drug Abuse (NIDA) reports that the availability of Buprenorphine treatment in doctors' office "may even prompt attempts to obtain treatment earlier."[7]

Ongoing research will continue to guide the path toward more effective drug treatment. Recent research from England found providing heroin as part of a treatment program showed better results than the use of methadone. Starting from our basic premise that each day out of the drug market represents a victory, policy makers should consider adopting any programs that increase an addict's days in treatment.

CHANGES FOR DRUG AFFLICTED NEIGHBORHOODS

Street drug dealing quickly destroys neighborhoods. Dealers and their customers bring public disorder and violence. Petty crime escalates, residents who complain are bullied and intimidated, property owners leave, and buildings fall into disrepair. Local businesses begin to suffer as fearful customers shun them, and those with resources escape (move) to a safer community. Community leaders demand action from the police who increase patrols, mount sting and buy-busts operations in the neighborhood. Arrests increase and drugs, money and weapons are confiscated but the problem persists.

There have been a number of community-police initiatives that have experienced some success against open-air drug markets. Literature on problem-oriented policing includes a number of strategies that have been used around the country with varying success. I have been a part of numerous neighborhood efforts to solve the problem and have seen some success. I am particularly impressed with the Citizens on Patrol Program which operates in my own neighborhood and has had a real deterrent effect on drug dealing, but a strategy to drive the dealers out of business has yet to be realized.

Customers are the lifeblood of the illegal drug market. Moving marijuana to the legitimate market eliminates roughly 40% of the dealers' customers. The loss of this volume of buyers shrinks the market considerably and, in and of itself, will reduce associated problems. Moving remaining addicts from the market to treatment will further shrink the market.

There are two other recommended policy steps that can effectively provide strong disincentives to customers seeking illegal drugs. The first is to equalize criminal penalties and risks for drug buyers and sellers. As the legislation implementing this change is passed, significant publicity on the change will enhance its effectiveness. In the current illegal market, the dealer assumes the bulk of the risks of arrest and prosecution. Increasing their risk of arrest will likely deter many drug buyers.

The second step is to enhance penalties for public drug transaction. Drug transactions in public heighten the physical risk for bystanders as well as contribute to neighborhood disorder. Unfortunately, nearly every day brings a news report about individuals caught in the crossfire stemming from drug deals. Enhanced penalties for public dealing would tend to drive these transactions indoors and thus reduce the crime and disorder accompanying the open-air markets.

The retail distribution of legalized marijuana would require close regulation. Currently, some neighborhoods struggle with problems stemming from bars and other businesses where disorderly patrons congregate. The potential for similar problems around licensed marijuana outlets is clear. Neighborhoods and communities must be given significant control and input into the number of outlets, operating hours, and other regulation controlling these operations. Responsible ownership that exerts strong control over its operation, both inside and outside, should be mandated. Those who fail to adequately control their operations and its patrons should have their license quickly rescinded. Regulations should ensure strong community input on both new licenses and renewals. Such regulations will help to ensure that license holders act as good neighbors.

WHERE TO FROM HERE?

In the days prior to GPS systems, travelers often stopped to ask for directions. Occasionally, they were met with a confused look and told "You can't get there from here." Government leaders at all levels have been lost in the morass of failed drug policy but while the path ahead appears uncertain, significant change can be accomplished.

On marijuana policy, the choices are stark. The medical marijuana movement continues to grow with New Jersey joining 14 other medical marijuana states in 2010. The federal government has, in essence, decided to withdraw from the medical marijuana issue, punting the issue to state legislatures. State legislative bodies now face three options. First, do nothing and continue to watch state and local government services be crushed under criminal justice costs and declining revenue; second, approve medical marijuana perhaps saving some governmental costs but allowing the development of an uncontrolled marijuana grey market; or three, take the step of moving marijuana to the legal market accompanied by substantial regulatory authority and significant taxing options. The "do nothing" option continues the enrichment of the criminal enterprises controlling marijuana. The medical marijuana option may have an impact on the illegal drug market but risks a citizenry exposed to a marketplace of fraudulent and unregulated products. The third option carries not only financial benefits to government but also directly undercuts the financial structure of the illegal drug market.

Accompanying legalization and supported by marijuana tax revenue should be a commitment to increasing drug treatment capacity, a renewed emphasis on drug prevention/education, and a significant increase in Drug Court funding. All these steps encroach on the illegal drug business by directly taking their customers out of the market.

The recommendations listed above target the illegal drug market but have the potential to deter alcohol and tobacco related problems as well. The emphasis on drug education and prevention programming targets alcohol and tobacco as well as other drugs. The cultural shift against tobacco will continue to generate increased regulation of tobacco use and the recent Federal legislation enabling FDA authority over tobacco products as well as the national emphasis on containing health care costs will accelerate this process.

Alcoholism continues to play a major role in the crime and social problems afflicting the country. Much of the policy prescription proposed will have a positive impact on these problems. In the 1970s, when I began work treating heroin addicts, we believed that drug addiction and alcoholism were completely different conditions. When treatment professionals began to recognize there was significant overlap in the two groups, the term "poly-drug users" came into vogue. Most of the addicted individuals using drugs today do not use a single drug to the exclusion of all others.

The policy steps listed aim to increase the number of addicts in treatment and lower the stigma associated with addiction. These are two key elements in the process. Reducing stigma will make it easier for alcoholics to seek treatment, shortening their addiction careers and minimizing the damage to their families and communities.

The criminal justice system will continue to be an important lever in moving all addicts, including alcoholics, into the treatment system. The success of Drug Courts has spawned specialized DWI Courts in several jurisdictions, and these programs have been effective with repeat DWI offenders as well as first offenders. As of the end of 2007, there were nearly 400 specialized DWI courts in operation in the United States.[8] The principles that underlie the success of Drug Courts will generalize to those whose primary drug of choice is alcohol.

Alcohol and tobacco will continue to pose a major challenge to policymakers. As both are solidly entwined in a regulatory control system, there exists an almost endless variety of tactics that could be deployed as the nature of alcohol/tobacco problems evolve.

Pharmaceutical diversion represents another challenge. Drug diversion, broadly defined, includes a wide variety of problems, from family members sharing prescription medicine, to addicted medical professionals feeding their own habits, to criminal enterprises selling stolen or counterfeit drugs in the illegal market. There is no simple solution to the varying issues included under the diversion umbrella. The inappropriate and potentially dangerous sharing of prescription drugs will almost certainly increase as the population ages and the costs of medicine continues to escalate. Strong patient education efforts on the part of the medical community represent the best chance to control this problem.

Doctor shoppers and addicts utilizing fraudulent prescriptions can avail themselves of the same options that all addicts will face when criminally charged. Drug Court type programs and closely monitored treatment will lead to positive outcomes for the majority of these offenders. Individuals who traffic in diverted prescription drugs are no different than street dealers slinging crack on city corners and should expect the same consequences.

CONCLUSION

Moving marijuana into a legal regulatory market and taking the other steps recommended will have significant positive benefits. More people in recovery from their addiction, a reduced number of drug offenders in our overcrowded prisons, lower health care costs and fewer neighborhoods ravaged by drug trafficking are just a few of the benefits that will come with drug law reform. Despite the potential, it is important to recognize that our drug-related problems, including street violence, will not be easily or quickly resolved.

Drug trafficking is a violent business and the people involved have a propensity for violence that is nearly incomprehensible to the average American. When I was a rookie police officer, I was dispatched to a shooting at a fast food restaurant. There had been a fight at a local nightclub and the dispute re-kindled in a nearby restaurant parking lot. Several officers responded and we were able to safely take the shooter into custody. I asked him what the dispute was all about. He told me that the expletive he had just shot had offered him a piece of gum as the two were standing next to each other at the club. The shooter took that as an insult, a statement that he had bad breath. In his mind, this was disrespect at a level that required a deadly response. Both the participants had significant drug offense histories and the media the next day described the shooting as "drug-related."

On another occasion, I was interviewing a shooter who had severely wounded a rival dealer in a street gunfight. I assumed it was a dispute over the drugs. "Naw," he told me, "the asshole scratched my car." These are incidents that are typical across the country and are a manifestation more of the violent tendencies of the individuals involved in the drug trade than they are of the nature of the drug market. If we disrupt and minimize the impact of the drug market, these violent individuals are not likely to easily transition to law-abiding citizens. Some of them will engage in other illegal activity and will continue to victimize the community until they are jailed or themselves made a homicide victim. We can, however, work towards a future where the illegal drug market no longer provides a financial incentive for violent behavior. Supplementing drug reform laws, social policies that improve economic opportunities, particularly in urban areas, may be our best chance of reducing the street violence that terrorizes so many of our communities.

The same sort of shift is likely on the international front. If we are successful, some of these organizations will move to other illegal, though less profitable, activities. They will adapt and diversify, moving into fraud, prostitution, human trafficking and other illegal activities. The drug trade will undoubtedly persist at some level. Much like a chronic disease, it will require ongoing management and control at the international, national and local level.

Changing the status of marijuana from illegal to legal will not be the end of problems related to that drug. One need only look at alcohol and tobacco to disabuse ourselves of the notion that changing the legal status of a drug will end related problems. There are significant benefits that will come with legalization but the nature of the drug problems in a legal structure will continue to provide challenges to policy makers.

The history of drug prohibition going back to alcohol prohibition through the 1920s is littered with policy failures. A common factor in that failure is the disconnect between the policy, the values, and the culture of the community. History is replete with examples of policy failures doomed by community opposition. Miron and Tetelbaum, writing on federal policy mandates, note that "A policy imposed from on high, especially one that is readily evaded and opposed by a large fraction of the citizenry, is virtually guaranteed to fail."[9] This is certainly an apt description of our current prohibition approach.

We need to engage in a national conversation on drug policy. The debate is likely to be heated and occasionally loud. Yet even the "shouting match" aspect described by Parloff can be a step toward common ground. Moving much of the decision-making on drug policy from the federal government to the states would be an action that conservatives should surely embrace. The movement toward treatment rather than jail for addicts and the end of a repressive and ineffective stance toward marijuana use would be met with liberal applause.

There is one overarching goal that can unite Americans behind a new drug policy paradigm. I believe that framing American drug policy in the context of disabling drug cartels is a goal that all Americans can enthusiastically support. It is drug money that is fueling Taliban insurgents in Afghanistan, funding Al-

Queda in Africa, that is arming drug gangs on the Mexican border and that is providing the financial support for the poisonous drug markets in our cities.

A drug policy that can stem the flow of dollars to the cartels that threaten us both internally and internationally would be welcome by Americans of every political stripe. It is past time to begin a conversation on the design and implementation of such a policy.

NOTES

1. Grant, Japhy (2010). "Is California High? New Pot Initiative Is Bad Policy." Retrieved from http://trueslant.com/japhygrant/2010/03/24/ on April 4, 2010.
2. Ibid.
3. Mills, James (1998), *The Hearing*. Warner Books, Inc., New York, NY. 67.
4. Dunston, Roger. (1997). "Gambling and Crime." California Research Bureau. Retrieved from http://www.library.ca.gov/CRB/97/03/crb97003.html. April 27, 2009.
5. FBI (2010). Crime in the United States, 2008. Retrieved from http://www.fbi.gov/ucr/cius2008/arrests/index.html.
6. Sullum, Jacob (2008, January). "Data: High Risk." *Reason Magazine*,
7. NIDA (2006) "Buprenorphine: Treatment for Opiate Addiction Right in the Doctor's Office." National Institute on Drug Abuse Research Update.
8. Huddleston, C. W., Marlowe, D. & Casebolt, R. (2008, May). Painting the Current Picture: A National Report Card On Drug Courts and Other Problem-Solving Court Programs In The United States. U.S. Department of Justice Bureau of Justice Assistance.
9. Miron, J. & Tetelbaum, E. (2009). "The Dangers of the Drinking Age." Retrieved from http://www.forbes.com/2009/04/15/lowering-legal-drinking-age-opinions-contributors-regulation.html.

Bibliography

Adlaf, E. M., Smart, R. G., & Canale, M. D. (1991). *Drug Use among Ontario Adults 1977-1991*. Toronto: Ontario Addiction Research Foundation.

A&E (2009). "A&E Network's Award-Winning Series "Intervention" Returns For A Seventh Season Monday, May 25 At 9pm Et/Pt." Released by A&E May 5, 2009.

Alcoholism Council of Cincinnati (January, 1981). *"The Drinking Driver Problem: Where to From Here"* A Report to the Board of Trustees of the Alcoholism Council of Cincinnati.

Anderson, Elijah. (1999) *Code of the Streets: Decency, Violence, and the Moral Life of the Inner City*. W.W. Norton and Company, New York, N.Y.

Associated Press, (2007, July 10). "Santa Barbara Loses Legal Effort To Dump Pot Law."

Barol, B. Prout, L. Fitzgerald, K., Katz, S. & King, P. (1986, July 28). "Cocaine Babies: Hooked at Birth." *Newsweek Magazine*.

Billeaud, J. (2008, January 12). "Kidnappings for Ransom Move North of the Border." *Cincinnati Enquirer*.

Blocker, J. (2006, February). "Did Prohibition Really Work? Alcohol Prohibition as a Public Health Innovation." *American Journal of Public Health*, 96(2): 239–241.

Bowden, Charles (2010). *Murder City*. Nation Books, New York, NY.

Bronstein, Hugh (2010, January 5). "Colombia Rebels, Al Qaeda in "Unholy" Drug Alliance." Reuters.com.

Burham, J.C. (1968). "Was Prohibition a Failure?" *Journal of Social History*, 1968-1969.

Burns, R. (2007 January 15). "Seizures of Cocaine Shipments Fall Off in '07." *Greenville News*.

Bureau of Justice Statistics. (2006, October). *Drug Use and Dependence, State and Federal Prisoners, 2004* [Data file]. Retrieved from http://www.ojp.usdoj.gov/bjs.
Bureau of Justice Statistics. (2003, December). *Violent Victimization of College Students: National Crime Victimization Survey 1995-2000* [Data file]. Retrieved from http://www.ojp.usdoj.gov/bjs.
Bureau of Justice Statistics. (1999, January). *Substance Abuse and Treatment, State and Federal Prisoners, 1999* [Data file]. Retrieved from http://www.ojp.usdoj.gov/bjs/pub.
Bureau of Justice Statistics (BJS). (1998). *Alcohol and Crime: An Analysis of National Data on the Prevalence of Alcohol Involvement in Crime.* Retrieved from http://www.ojp.usdoj.gov/bjs/pub/pdf/ac.pdf.
CBS News Crimesider: David Hartley Update. (2011) http://www.cbsnews.com/8301-504083_162-20020054-504083.html. downloaded 6/15/2011.
Callahan, Rick. (2009). "Colleges Urged To Mellow On Pot." Cincinnati Enquirer (AP), p. A9. May 17, 2009.
Carter, S. A. & Barrera, E. (2006, February 28). "Slayings Tied to Cartels." *San Bernadino County News.*
Carter, S. A. (2009, March 27). "Hezbollah Uses Mexican Drug Routes into U.S." *Washington Times.*
Carey, S. M., Finigan, M., Crumpton. D., & Waller, M. (2006). "California Drug Courts: Outcomes, Costs and Promising Practices." An overview of phase II in a statewide study. *Journal of Psychoactive Drugs, SARC Supplement* 3, 345-356.
Castillo, E. Eduardo. (2010) "Gunmen Kill 15 Mexican Officers." Associated Press, June 15, 2010.
Caulkins, J. P., Reuter, P.H., Iguchi, M.Y. & Chiesa, J. (2003). "Drug Use and Drug Policy Futures: Insights from a Colloquium."Retrieved from http://www.rand.org/pubs/issue_papers/IP246/.
Centers for Disease Control and Prevention (CDC). (1997, May 23). "Smoking-Attributable Mortality and Years of Potential Life Lost: United States, 1984." *Morbidity and Mortality Weekly Report, 46*(20). Retrieved from http://www.cdc.gov/mmwr/preview/mmwrhtml/00047690.htm.
Central Intelligence Agency. (2007). *Field Listing: Elicit drugs* [Data file]. Retrieved from http://www.cia.gov/library/publications/the-world-factbook/.
Choose Responsibility (2000). "Arguments Against Legal Age 21," http://www.chooseresponsibility.org/against_legal_age. Downloaded 4/1/09.
Chron.com (2011). "More drug violence, plus reports of 8500 orphans in Juarez." Retrieved from HTTP://blog.chron.com/newswatch/2011/02
Clark, N. H. (1976). *Deliver Us From Evil: An Interpretation of American Prohibition.* New York, NY: Norton Publishing.

Cohen, Peter, and Reinarman, Craig. (1999) "Human Nature – A Response to Larry Collins." *Foreign Affairs Magazine* Website. http://www.foreignaffairs.org/. Downloaded September 13, 2009.

Cohen, Peter. (2006). "Looking at the UN, Smelling a Rat." *CEDRO*, www.cedro-uva.org/. Downloaded September 30, 2009: 6-7.

Cole, Jack. (2009) *This is Not a War on Drugs—it's a War on People.* http://leap.cc/cms/index.php?name=Content&pid=29. Downloaded 3/13/2009.

Collins, Larry. (1999). "Holland's Half-Baked Drug Experiment." *Foreign Affairs*, Vol. 78, No. 3. May/June,1999. New York, N.Y. http://www.foreignaffairs.org/. Downloaded September 13, 2009.

Conery, Ben. (2009) "Marijuana Found in Another National Park." *The Washington Times.* August 29, 2009. Retrieved from http://www.washingtontimes.com/news/2009/aug/29/.

CSPI (1996), Paying *the* Piper: The Effect of Industry Funding on Alcohol Prevention Priorities. Center for Science in the Public Interest, Washington, D.C. http://www.cspinet.org/booze/ppstudy.html. Downloaded August 25, 2009.

Davis, Mark. (2008, March 12) "Buckley, Legal Drugs and My Evolving View." Dallas Morning News.

DEA, (2003) *Speaking Out Against Drug Legalization*, U.S. Department of Justice, Drug Enforcement Administration, May, 2003.

Degenhardt, Louisa; Christopher Hallam; and Dave Bewley-Taylor. (2009) *Comparing The Drug Situation Across Countries: Problems, Pitfalls And Possibilities*. The Beckley Foundation, Sydney, Australia, September, 2009.

Devine, J. (2009, July 17). "A Brief History of DWI Law." Retrieved from http://ezinearticles.com/?A-Brief-History-of-DWI-Law&id=1335561.

Dick, Danielle and Agrawal, Arpana (2008). "The Genetics of Alcohol and Other Drug Dependence." Alcohol Research & Health, Vol 31, No. 2. P. 111, National Institute on Alcohol Abuse and Alcoholism (NIAAA).

Diehl, H. (1969). *Tobacco and Your Health.* New York, NY: McGraw-Hill Book Co.

Drug Policy Around the World (2009). ttp://www.drugpolicy.org/global/. Downloaded 7/29/2009.

DUKE Today (November 22, 2004). "Smoking's Real Cost Reaches $40 Per Pack Over Lifetime, Duke Study Concludes." Duke Today, November 22, 2004. Retrieved from http://today.duke.edu/2004/11/costofsmoking_1104.html

Duncan, D.F., & Nicholson, T. (1997). "Dutch Drug Policy: A Model for America?" *Journal of Health and Social Policy, 8*(3), 1-15.

Dunston, Roger. (1997). "Gambling and Crime." California Research Bureau. Retrieved from http://www.library.ca.gov/CRB/97/03/crb97003.html. April 27, 2009.

Economist, (2009). "Portugal's Drug Policy: Treating, not Punishing." Lisbon, August 27, 2009.

EMCDDA (2006). *Annual Report 2006: The State of the Drugs Problem in Europe*. Office for Official Publications of the European Communities, Luxembourg.

Engleman, Larry. (1979). *Intemperance: The Lost War Against Liquor.* New York, NY: Free Press, XI.

Engelsman, E. L. (1989) "Dutch Policy on the Management of Drug-Related Problems." *British Journal of Addiction.* 1989; 84: 211-218.

Eskenazi, Joe. (2010) "Legalize It: Ammiano to Introduce Legislation Monday to Allow Pot – and Tax It." San Franciso Weekly .http://blogs.sfweekly.com/thesnitch/2009/02/legalize_it_ammiano_to_intro du.php downloaded April 11.

Erickson, P. G., & Alexander, B. K. (1989). Cocaine and addictive liability. *Social Pharmacology*, *3*, 249-270.

Fazey, Cindy. (2003) "The UN Drug Policies and the Prospect for Change." http://www.fuoriluogo.it/arretrati/2003/apr_17_en.htm. Retrieved November 3 2009.

FBI (2009). Special Agent Frequently Asked Questions. http://www.fbijobs.gov/114.asp. Downloaded May 9, 2009.

FBI (2010). Crime in the United States, 2008. Retrieved from http://www.fbi.gov/ucr/cius2008/arrests/index.html.

Fainaru, Steve, and William Booth. (2009) "Cartels Face an Economic Battle." Washington Post, October 7, 2009. http://www.washingtonpost.com/wp-dyn/content/article/2009/10/06/AR2009100603847.html. Retrieved 10/30/2009.

Fletcher, Bennett and Chandler, Redonna (2009). "Principles of Drug Abuse Treatment for Criminal Justice Populations." National Institute of Drug Abuse. http://www.nida.nih.gov. Retrieved October 29, 2009.

Frank, Deborah, M.D. (2002) Testimony before the United States Sentencing Commission. February 21, 2002.

Gambrell, Jon (2009, February11). "Candy-Flavored Meth Targets New Users." Associated Press. Retrieved from http://www.cbsnews.com/stories/ 2007/05/02/health/ main2752266.shtml

Gathright, Alan (2009, November 3). "Breckenridge Pot Legalization Creates Big Buzz." TheDenverChannel.com, http://www.thedenverchannel.com/ news/21515178/detail.html, Retrieved September 9, 2011.

Gettleman, Jeffery. "In Baltimore, Slogan Collides with Reality." *NY Times*, September 2, 2003.

Gettman, John. (2007) "Lost Taxes and Other Costs of Marijuana Laws." The Bulletin of Cannabis Reform. www.Drugscience.org, downloaded May 11, 2009.

Glusing, Jens (2007, February 28. "Violence in Rio de Janeiro: Child Soldiers in the Drug War." Retrieved from http://www.essex.ac.uk/armedcon/story_id/ 000448. htmlsjpigal online, 3/2/2007.

Goodman, Joshua. (2007) "U.S. Cocaine Prices Drop, Purity Increases." Associated Press, April 27, 2007.

Gorner, Jeremy (2009, June2). "No bail in slayings of 3 found in car." Chicago Tribune Online. Retrieved from http://articles.chicagobreakingnews.com/2011-06-02/news/29614708_1_drug-trafficking-crew-segura-rodriguez-and-augustin-toscano-slayings\

Grant, Japhy (2010). "Is California High? New Pot Initiative Is Bad Policy." Retrieved from http://trueslant.com/japhygrant/2010/03/24/ on April 4, 2010.

Greater Dallas Area Council on Alcoholism and Drug Abuse. (2006). *Alcohol: Facts, statistics, resources and impairment charts.* Retrieved from http://www.gdcada.org/statistics/alcohol.htm.

Greenwald, Glenn. (2009). *Drug Decriminalization in Portugal: Lessons for Creating Fair and Successful Drug Policies.* CATO Institute. Washington, D.C., 3.

Grillo, Joan. (2009) "Mexico's New Drug Law May Set an Example." *TIME.com*, August 26, 2009. http://TIME.com. Downloaded 8/26/2009.

Hamilton, Matthew (2010). "18-Wheeler's Load Included Cucumbers, 105 Pounds of Cocaine." The News Star, April 14, 2010. Retrieved from http://www.thenewsstar.com/article/20100414.

Hampton, Deon and Adcock, Clifton (2010). "Police Seize 1,500 Pounds of Marijuana." Tulsa World, April 17, 2010. Retrieved from http://www.tulsaworld.com/news/.

Hanson, David.(2009) *Dry Counties.* Alcohol Problems and Solutions. http://www2.potsdam.edu/hansondj/controversies/1140551076.html. Downloaded 3/11/2009.

Harlow, J. (2007, November 11). "Drug Smugglers Use Submarines." *Times Online.* Retrieved from http://www.timesonline.co.uk/tol/news/world/us_and_americas/article2848238.ec.

Harm Reduction Coalition (2009*). Principles of Harm Reduction.* http://www.harmreduction.org/. Downloaded August 25, 2009.

Harwood, H. (2000, December). *Updating Estimates of the Economic Costs of Alcohol Abuse in the United States: Estimates, Update Methods, and Data.* Rockville, MD: National Institutes of Health.

Harocopos, Alex and Hough, Mike. (2005) *Drug Dealing in Open-Air Markets.* Department of Justice, Office of Community Oriented Policing. Washington, D.C.

Helms, Nat. (2009) "Army Report: Drug Cartels, Terrorists Infiltrate U.S." *Newsmax.com*, June 5, 2009. http://www.newsmax.com/newsfront/mexico_border_fence/2009/06/05/222148.html?utm_medium=RSS. Retrieved November 4, 2009.

Huddleston, C. West, Marlowe, Douglas, Casebolt, Rachel. (2008) "Painting the Current Picture: A National Report Card on Drug Courts and Other Problem-Solving Court Programs in the United States." Bureau of Justice Assistance, Department of Justice, May 2008.

Hughes, Caitlan and Stevens, Alex. (2007). "The Effects of Decriminalization of Drugs in Portugal." *The Beckley Foundation*, www.internationaldrug policy.net. Downloaded September 15, 2009.

IDPC (2009). "The Netherlands Reviews its Tolerant Approach to Drug Policy." *International Drug Policy Consortium*, http://www.idpc.net/alerts/review-dutch-drugs-policy-summary. Downloaded September 13, 2009.

IDT (2006). Institute on Drugs and Drug Addiction of Portugal. "The National Situation Relating to Drugs and Dependency," 2005 Annual Report (2006).

INFOplease.com (2011). "Cigarette Consumption, United States, 1900-2007." Retrieved from http://www.infoplease.com/ipa/A0908700.html

Jane's Information Group. (2006 November 15). "Afghanistan's Narcotics-Fuelled Insurgency." Retrieved from

Jenkins, Austin (2009, January 22). "Federal Prosecutors Crack Down on Addicted Doctors." OPB News, Retrieved from

Johnson, Elaine (1995). "Cheers for the Designated Driver Program," Safety and Health, The National Safety Council, Itaska, IL, 1995.

Johnson, Shelley and Latessa, Edward. (2000) "The Hamilton County Drug Court: Outcome Evaluation Findings." Center for Criminal Justice Research, University of Cincinnati. July, 2000.

Johnston, L. D., O'Malley, P. M., Bachman, J. G., & Schulenberg, J. E. (2011). *Monitoring the Future national survey results on drug use, 1975-2010. Volume I: Secondary school students*. Ann Arbor: Institute for Social Research, The University of Michigan, 734 pp.

Johnston, L.C., O'Malley, P.M., Bachman, J.G. & Schulenberg, J.E. (2007, December 11). "Overall, Illicit Drug Use by American Teens Continues Gradual Decline in 2007." *University of Michigan News Service: Ann Arbor*. Available from http://www.monitoringthefuture.org.

Jojola, Jeremy and Kappus, Matthew. "Medical Marijuana Grower to Begin Distribution." *KOB.com*, posted 6/3/2009. http://www.kob.com/article/stories/S961683.shtml. Retrieved November 2, 2009.

Kane, John. "Policy is Not a Synonym for Justice." In *The New Prohibition: Voices of Dissent Challenge the Drug War*. Edited by Sheriff Bill Masters, St. Louis: Accurate Press, 2004, Chapter 5, p. 45.

Kandel, D. B., Murphy, D., & Karus, D. (1985). "Cocaine Use in Young Adulthood: Patterns of Use and Psychosocial Correlates." In N. J. Kozel and E. H. Adams (Eds.). *Cocaine Use in America: Epidemiologic and Clinical Perspectives*. Washington, DC: U.S. Government Printing Office: 76-110.

Kittrels, Alonzo (2006, November 27). "We've made amazing progress in the last century." Retrieved from http/www.gamehavoc.com/showthread.php?17247

Knickerbocker, B. (2005, July 15). "Meth's Rising U.S. Impact." *The Christian Science Monitor*. Retrieved from http://www.csmonitor.com/2005/0715/p03s01-ussc.html.

Kramer, Tom; Jelsma, Martin; Blickman, Tom. (2009, January) *Withdrawal Symptoms in the Golden Triangle: A Drugs Market in Disarray.* Transnational Institute, Amsterdam, Netherlands. P. 25.

Lacey, Marc (2009). "In Mexico, Ambivalence on a Drug Law." *The New York Times*, New York, NY. August 23, 2009

Larkin, Jack (1988). *The reshaping of everyday life, 1790-1840.* New York, NY: Harper & Row, 295.

LEAP (2010.) "End Prohibition Now Slide Show." Retrieved from http://www.google.com/search?q=Whites+constitute+72%25+of+all+drug+users+in+the&ie=utf-8&oe=utf-8&aq=t&rls=org.mozilla:en-US:official&client=firefox-a

Lender, M.E. & Martin, James K. (1987). *Drinking in America: A History.* New York, NY: Free Press, 205.

Lershner, Alan. (2005). "Why Should We Treat Addicts Anyway? The Solution We Refuse to Use." National Institute on Drug Abuse (NIDA), Director's page. http://www.nida.nih.gov/. Retrieved 10/24/2009.

Lershner, A. (2001, March). The Essence of Drug Addiction. *National Institute of Drug Abuse.* Retrieved from http://www.drugabuse.gov/Published_Articles/Essence.html.

Lillis, Mike. (2009) "Congress Looks to Lift Two-Decade Ban on Federal Needle Exchange Funds." The Washington Independent (online), July 9, 2009.

Local12 (2011) http://www.local12.com/news/local/story/Man-Murdered-in-Over-the-Rhine-While-Holding/ElMZQY5h_kWujazHOXLauA.cspx. May 18, 2011

Lowery, Brandon. "Marijuana Machines Could Be Cure For Inconvenience." L.A. Daily News, on-line edition, 1/29/2009. http://labs.daylife.com/journalist/brandon_lowrey. Retrieved November 2, 2009.

Lueck, T. J. (2007, January 8). "As Newark Mayor Readies Crime Fight, Toll Rises." *The New York Times.* Retrieved from http://www.nytimes.com/2007/01/08/nyregion/08newark.html

MMWR Weekly (May 22, 2009). "Federal and State Cigarette Excise Taxes – United States, 1995-2009," Center for Disease Control, Retrieved from http://www.cdc.gov/mmwr/preview/mmwrhtml/mm5819a2.htm

Marlowe, D.B. (2006). "Judicial Supervision of Drug-Abusing Offenders." *Journal of Psychoactive Drugs, SARC Supplement* 3, 323-331.

Mattingly, David. (2009, May8). "Minority Youngsters Dying Weekly on Chicago's Streets." Retrieved from McGrew, J. (2008). *History of Tobacco Regulation.* National Commission on Marihuana and Drug Abuse. Retrieved from http://www.druglibrary.org/Schaffer/LIBRARY/studies/nc/nc2b.htm.

McWilliams, Jeremiah (2009). "Budweiser Launches New Responsibility Campaign." St. Louis Dispatch, May 26, 2009.

Michaels, Jim. "Mexican Military Gets US Advice." Cincinnati Enquirer. April 8, 2010, A6.

Miller, S. (2008, November 11). 'Bolivia, Ecuador, Venezuela Evict U.S. Drug Warriors." *The Christian Science Monitor.* Retrieved from http://www.csmonitor.com.

Mills, James (1998), *The Hearing.* Warner Books, Inc., New York, NY

Miron, Jeffery and Tetelbaum, Elina. (2009). "The Dangers of the Drinking Age." http://www.forbes.com/2009/04/15/lowering-legal-drinking-age-opinions-contributors-regulation.html. Retrieved November 4, 2009.

Miron, Jeffrey.(2004) "Liberal versus Libertarian Views on Drug Legalization," Published in *The New* Masters, Bill. (2004). *Prohibition: Voices of Dissent Challenge the Drug War,* Accurate Press.

Montague, P (Ed.). "America's Secret Drug War." *Third World Traveler.* Retrieved from http://www.thirdworldtraveler.com/CIA/secret_war.html.

Moore, Solomon. (2009) "Fewer Blacks in Prison for Drugs." N.Y. Times, April 14, 2009.

Morgan, J. P. & Zimmer, L. (1997). "The Social Pharmacology of Smokeable Cocaine: Not All It's Cracked Up to Be." In. C. Reinarman and H. Levine (Eds.). *Crack in America: Demon Drugs and Social Justice.* Regents of the University of California.

Morse, Janet (2009, March 7). "Twin pediatricians face charges of molestation." Cincinnati Enquirer, Retrieved from http://www.enquirer.com/editions/pdf/KY_CE_070309.pdf

Musto, David (1987). The American Disease, Oxford University Press, New York, NY.

Nahmais, R. (2007, November 2). "Expert: Hamas, Hezbollah Cells may be Active in Mexico." *Ynet News.* Retrieved From http://www.ynetnews.com.

National Commission on Law Observance and Enforcement. (1931, January 7). *Report on the Enforcement of the Prohibition Laws of the United States.* Washington D.C.: U.S. Government Printing Office.

National Council for Crime Prevention (2000). "The Criminalization of Narcotic Drug Misuse -- An Evaluation of Criminal Justice System Measures" (English summary), Stockholm, 42.

National Drug Intelligence Center, (NDIC) (2010). *National Drug Threat Assessment, 2010.* National Drug Intelligence Center, Department of Justice, Washington, D.C.

National Drug Intelligence Center (NDIC). (2006, June 5). *Fentanyl: Situation Report.* Retrieved from http://www.justice.gov/ndic/srs/20469/index.htm.

National Drug Intelligence Center (NDIC0) (2004, November) "Pharmaceuticals Drug Threat Assessment." Retrieved from http://www.justice.gov/ndic/pubs11/11449/diversion.htm

National Highway Traffic Safety Administration. (2009). *The Visual Detection of DWI Motorists.* Available from http://www.nhtsa.gov.

NSDUH (2009). National Survey on Drug Use and Health. http://www.oas.samhsa.gov/. Retrieved October 22, 2009. Table 1.12B.

National Institute on Alcohol Abuse and Alcoholism (NIAAA), (2009). "Apparent Per Capita Ethanol Consumption for the United States, 1850–2006.

(Gallons of Ethanol, Based on Population age 15 and Older.)" http://alcoholism.about.com.

National Institute on Drug Abuse (NIDA) (2006) "Buprenorphine: Treatment for Opiate Addiction Right in the Doctor's Office." National Institute on Drug Abuse Research Update.

National Institute on Drug Abuse (NIDA) (2004). *NIDA Info Facts: Lessons from Prevention Research*. National Institute of Drug Abuse, Washington, D.C., June, 2009. http://www.nida.nih.gov/infofacts/. Retrieved October 20, 2009.

National Institute on Drug Abuse (NIDA) (2008). NIDA Info Facts: Treatment Statistics. National Institute of Drug Abuse, Washington, D.C., June, 2008. http://www.nida.nih.gov/infofacts. Retrieved June 15, 2009.

National Institute on Drug Abuse (NIDA). (2006, July). "Tobacco Addiction." *NIDA Research Report Series, 06-4342*. Retrieved from http://www.nida.nih.gov/PDF/TobaccoRRS_v16.pdf.

National Institute on Drug Abuse (NIDA). (2004, November). "Cocaine Use and Addiction." *NIDA Research Report Series, 99-4342*. Retrieved from http://www.nida.nih.gov/PDF/RRCocaine.pdf.

National Institute on Drug Abuse. (NIDA) (2005, July). "Marijuana Abuse." *NIDA Research Report Series, 05-3859*. Retrieved from http://www.drugabuse.gov/PDF/RRMarijuana.pdf.

National Institute on Drug Abuse. (NIDA) (2009, July). *NIDA Infofacts: Marijuana*. Retrieved from http://www.drugabuse.gov/infofacts/marijuana.html.

National Institute on Drug Abuse (NIDA) (2009, September) NIDA infofacts: Heroin {Data file}. Retrieved from http://www.nida.nih.gov/infofacts/heroin.html"

National Institute on Drug Abuse (NIDA) (2005, May). "Heroin Abuse and Addiction." *NIDA Research Report Series, 05-5165*. Retrieved from http://www.nida.nih.gov/PDF/RRHeroin.pdf.

National Institute on Drug Abuse (NIDA), (2006, September). Methamphetamine abuse and addiction, *NIDA Research Report Series*, 06-4210. Retrieved from http://www.nida.nih.gov/PDF/RRMetham.pdf

National Institute on Drug Abuse (NIDA) (2009). *NIDA Info Facts: Crack and Cocaine*. National Institute of Drug Abuse, Washington, D.C., June, 2009. http://www.nida.nih.gov/infofacts/. Retrieved October 12, 2009.

Newton, Paula. (2009) "Study Touts Treating Heroin Addicts with Heroin." *CNN News*, October 20, 2009. http://www.cnn.com/2009/HEALTH/10/20/treating.with.heroin/index.html#cnnSTCText. Retrieved October 29, 2009.

Ohio Resource Network for Safe and Drug Free Schools and Communities. (2006, May 26). "'Bad' Heroin Found After Epidemic of Overdoses." *Ohio Early Warning Alert*. Retrieved from http://www.ebasedprevention.org/files/Heroin_Alert_Supplement.pdf.

Para, N. (2007, February 7). "Seven State Workers Slain in Acapulco." *Associated Press*.

Parekh, R. (2005, February 28). "Companies fight tobacco use to lower health care costs." Business Insurance, 39(9), 4-5.
Parker, Kathleen. (2009, February 13) *Sometimes a Smoke is Just a Smoke.* Postwriters.com
Parloff, Roger. (2009). "How Marijuana Became Legal." Fortune Magazine, September 18, 2009. On-line edition, http://rss.cnn.com/rss/magazines_fortune.rss. Retrieved November2, 2009.
Peele, Stanton & DeGrandpre, Richard. (1998). Cocaine and the Concept of Addiction: Environmental Factors in Drug Compulsions." Addiction Research, Retrieved from http://www.peele.net/lib/cocaine.html
Police Executive Research Forum. (2006). *"A Gathering Storm – Violent Crime in America."* Retrieved from http://www.policeforum.org.
Porter, Anders. (2008). "Sweden's Tough Stance on Drugs up for Debate." March 23, 2008. Downloaded from http://www.sweden.se/eng/Home/Work-live/Government-politics/Reading/Not-so-user-friendly-debating-Swedish-drug-policy/wede.
Proctor, R.N. (1997). "The Nazi War on Tobacco: Ideology, Evidence, and Possible Cancer Consequences." Bull History Med, 71(3): 435–88.
Punch, M. (1985*) Conduct Unbecoming: The Social Construction of Police Deviance and Control.* London: Tavistock, 1985.
Rabinowitz, N. (2008). "Boston Commission Votes to Ban Cigar and Hookah bars, End Tobacco Sale on College Campuses." *Associated Press.* Retrieved from http://www.chicagotribune.com/news/nationworld/sns-ap- smoking-bar-ban9b,0, 1404279.
Rahtz, Howard (2001*). Community-Oriented Policing Handbook.* Monsey, NY. Criminal Justice Press.
Rueter, Peter and Caulkins, Jonathan. (2009) "An Assessment of Drug Incarceration and Foreign Interventions." Testimony before the House Oversight and Government Reform Committee, May 19, 2009.
Reuter, Peter; Trautmann, Franz; Pacula, Rosalie Liccardo;, Kilmer, Beau; Gageldonk, Andre; van der Gouwe, Daan. (2009) "Assessing Changes in Global Drug Problems, 1998-2000." The Rand Corporation.
Rickard, E. (2001, July 1). *How D*ry *We Were: The Repeal of P*rohibition. Retrieved from http://www.november.org/Prohibition/.
Robins, L.N., Helzer, J.E., Hesselbrock., M & Wish, E. (1980). "Vietnam Veterans Three Years After Vietnam: How Our Study Changed Our View Of Heroin." In L. Brill & C. Winick (Eds.). *Yearbook of Substance Use and Abuse.* New York: Human Science Press.
Robins, L.N., Davis, D.H. & Nurco, D.N.(1974). "How Permanent Was Vietnam Drug Addiction?" *American Journal of Public Health, 64* (Suppl), 38-43.
Robinson, Matthew B. and Renee G. Scherlen. (2007) *Lies, Damned Lies, and Drug War Statistics: A Critical Analysis of Claims Made by the Office of National Drug Control Policy*, State University of New York Press, New York, 2007.

Sakal, Mike. (2011, March 5). "Chandler police link beheading to theft of marijuana from Mexican cartel." East Valley Tribune.com Retrieved from http://www.eastvalleytribune.com/local/cop_shop/article_4dba9618-4540-11e0-98da-001cc4c03286.html

Samuels, David. (2009). "How Medical Marijuana is Transforming the Pot Industry." *New Yorker Magazine*. July 28, 2009.

Sanchez, Matt. (2009) "Mexican Drug Cartels Armed To the Hilt, Threatening National Security." *Fox News.com*, February 4, 2009. http://www.foxnews.com/story/0,2933,487911,00.html. Retrieved November 4, 2009.

Sandoval, E., Parascandola, R. and McShane, L. (2010, December 2) Drugs and guns are killing New York- two-thirds of murder victims are black, drugs involved." N.Y Daily News. Retrieved from http://articles.nydailynews.com/2010-12-02/news/27082935_1_murder-victims-drug-killings-murder-rate/2

Schaffer, Clifford. (2009) *Basic Facts about the War on Drugs*. Downloaded April 2, 2009.

Science Serving Society (2009). BAC Calculator. Retrieved from http://www.scienceservingsociety.com.

Sinclair, A. (1964). *Era of Excess: A Social History of the Prohibition Movement*. New York, NY: Harper and Row.

Spector, Joseph (2009). "New York passes drug law reform." Retrieved from http://www.poughkeepsiejournal.com/section/news

SRNNews.com, March 4 2011, "Drug Debate Apparent motive in Tacoma Homicide." Retrieved from http://srnnews.townhall.com/news/us/2011/03/04/drug_debate_apparent_motive_in_tacoma_homicide

Stenihauer, Jennifer. (2002) "Bloomberg Says He Regrets Marijuana Remarks." N.Y. Times. On-line Edition, April 10, 2002.

Strobel, W. P. (2009, March 27). "Clinton Says US Shares Responsibility for Mexico's Drug Violence." *The Christian Science Monitor*. Retrieved from http://www.csmonitor.com/2009/0327/p99s01-woam.html.

Stogel, S. (2004, July 14). "Al-Qaida has Nuclear Weapons Inside U.S." *NewsMax*. Available from http://www.newsmax.com/index.html.

Stroup, Keith. (2004) "Drug War Briefs: Voters Nationwide Embrace Marijuana Law Reform Proposals." National Organization For Reform of Marijuana Laws (NORML). December 1, 2004.

Substance Abuse and Mental health Services Administration. SAMSA (2009) Results from the 2008 National Survey on Drug Use and Health: National Findings (Office of Applied Studies, NSDUH Series H-36, HHS Publication No. SMA 09-4434. Rockville, MD.

Sullum, Jacob (2008, January). "Data: High Risk." *Reason Magazine*,

Surgeon General's Advisory Committee on Smoking and Health. (1964). "Smoking and Health." Public Health Service Publication No. 1103. United States: Public Health Service. Office of the Surgeon General, 196.

Tavares, LV, Graça, PM, Martins, O & Asensio, M (2005). *External and Independent Evaluation of the "National Strategy for the Fight Against*

Drugs" and of the "National Action Plan for the Fight Against Drugs and Drug Addiction – Horizon 2004." Portuguese National Institute of Public Administration, Lisbon.

Teaching with Documents: The Volstead Act. (2009) Retrieved from http://www.historicaldocuments.com/VolsteadAct.htm.

TheDenverChannel.Com (2009). "Breckenridge Votes To Legalize Marijuana." http://www.thedenverchannel.com/news/21515178/detail.html. Retrieved 11/4/2009.

The Sentencing Project (2009). "Federal Crack Cocaine Sentencing." Retrieved from http://sentencingproject.org/doc/publications/dp_CrackBriefingSheet.pdf

Tierra, M. (2007, June). Brief History and Culture of Tobacco. Retrieved from http://www.planetherbs.com/theory/brief-history-and-culture-of-tobacco.html.

Thompson, Cheryl. (2009, January 15). "Internet Experts Testify About Illegal Drug Sales." *Pharmacy News*. Retrieved from http://www.ashp.org/menu/News/PharmacyNews/NewsArticle.aspx?id=2078

Thompson, Ginger (2011). "US drug agents launder profits of Mexican cartels." *Cincinnati Enquirer*, A7, December 4, 2011.

Transform, (2006). "After the War on Drugs: Options for Control." *Transform Drug Policy Foundation*. www.tdpf.org.uk. Downloaded October 8, 2009.

USA Today (2010, September 14). "Illegal Drug Use Up Sharply." USA Today. Retrieved from http://www.usatoday.com/news/world/2010-09-14

USA Today (2008, January 3). "U.S. Expects Record Poppy Crop in Afghanistan." Retrieved from http://www.usatoday.com/news/world/2008-01-02-afghanistan-poppy_N.htm.

UNITED NATIONS OFFICE ON DRUGS AND CRIME. (1998). *ECONOMIC AND SOCIAL CONSEQUENCES OF DRUG ABUSE AND ILLICIT TRAFFICKING*. NEW YORK, NY: UNODCCP. RETRIEVED FROM http://www.unodc.org/pdf/technical_series_1998-01-01_1.pdf.

United Nations Office on Drugs and Crime. (2007). *2007 World Drug Report* [Data file]. Available from http://www.unodc.org/.

United Nations Office for Drug Control (1999). *Global Illicit Drug Trends*. United Nations Publication (ISBN 92-1-148122-8.

United Nations on Drugs and Crime, 2007. RETRIEVED FROM http://www.unodc.org/pdf/technical_series_1998-01-01_1.pdf.

United Nations Office on Drugs and Crime (2007). *Sweden's Successful Drug Policy: A Review of the Evidence*. United Nations, New York, NY, 12.

United States Sentencing Commission. (2002) *Report to Congress: Cocaine and Federal Sentencing Policy*, May 2002. http://www.druglibrary.org/schaffer/library/basicfax.htm, 45.

Vidal, G. (1972). *Homage to Daniel Shays: Collected essays 1952-1972*. New York, NY: Random House, 374.

Villalba, Oscar (2010). "Officials Say Gunmen Kill Seventeen at Party in Mexico." Associated Press, July 18, 2010. Retrieved from http://news.yahoo.com/s/ap/20100718/.

Vos, S. (2008, September 5). "Putting a Price on Smoking." *The Herald-Leader.* Retrieved from http://www.kentucky.com/181/story/514712.html.

Wagenaar, Alexander, Salois, Matthew & Komro, Kelli. (2009) *Effects of Beverage Alcohol Price and Tax Levels on Drinking: A Meta-Analysis of 1003 Estimates from 112 Studies.* Addiction, Volume 104, Issue 2. January 15, 2009: 179-190.

Wagenaar, Alexander, Maldonado-Molina, Mildred, Wagenaar, Bradley. (2007) "Effects of Alcohol Tax Increases on Alcohol-Related Disease Mortality in Alaska: Mime-Series Analyses from 1976 to 2004." American Journal of Public Health, http://www.ajph.org/cgi/content/abstract/AJPH.2007.131326v1?maxtoshow=&HI. Accessed 3/13/09.

Wagenaar AC. (1993) "Minimum Drinking Age and Alcohol Availability to Youth: Issues and Research Needs." Hilton ME, Bloss G, eds. *Economics and the Prevention of Alcohol-Related Problems.* National Institute on Alcohol Abuse and Alcoholism (NIAAA) Research Monograph No. 25, NIH Pub. No. 93-3513. Bethesda, MD: NIAAA; 1993:175-200.

Wagner, S. (1971). *Cigarette Country.* New York, NY: Praeger Publishers.

Weathers, W. (2007, January 13). "Homicide Record Just Got Worse." *Cincinnati Post*, p. B1.

Welch, William. (2009). "Booming Medical Pot Sales Concern Officials." *USA Today*, September 30, 2009, On-Line Edition. http://www.usatoday.com/news/nation/2009-09-29-medical-marijuana_N.htm. Downloaded October 14, 2009.

WHO (2004). Effectiveness of Sterile Needle and Syringe Programming in Reducing HIV/AIDS among Injecting Drug Users. World Health Organization, Switzerland, 28.

Wikipedia (2009) "Single Convention on Narcotic Drugs" http://en.wikipedia.org/wiki/Single_Convention_on_Narcotic_Drugs#Influence_on_domestic_legislation. Retrieved 11/3/2009.

Wikipedia (2009). "Alcohol Laws of the United States." http://en.wikipedia.org/wiki/Alcohol_laws_of_the_United_States_by_state. Downloaded 3/13/2009.

Wikipedia (2011). "Anti-Smoking Movement."(2011) Retrieved from: http://en.wikipedia.org/wiki/Anti-tobaccomovementinnazigermany.

Will, George. (2009, October 29). "Gil Kerlikowske's Reality Check In The Drug War." The Washington Post Retrieved from http://www.washingtonpost.com/wp-dyn/content/article/2009/10/28/AR2009102803801.html

Winkelman, R., Cannon, T. & Powell, J. *Alcohol Biology 105.* Retrieved from Lecture Notes Online Web site: http//www.mc.edu.campus/users/ rhamilto/BIOl105/Alcoholppt.

Zapotosky, White and Klein (2011, February). "Portraits of the 16 Killed This Year in Prince George's County." *Washington Post.*

Zimring, F. & Hawkins, G. (1992). *The Search for Rational Drug Control.* New York, NY: Cambridge.